And The Streets Are Paved
With Gold

And The Streets Are Paved With Gold

Harold Weiss

Writer's Showcase
San Jose New York Lincoln Shanghai

And The Streets Are Paved With Gold

Writer's Showcase
an imprint of iUniverse, Inc.

For information address:
iUniverse, Inc.
5220 S. 16th St., Suite 200
Lincoln, NE 68512
www.iuniverse.com

ISBN: 0-595-23400-3

Printed in the United States of America

To my wonderful parents, Sylvie and Mendel, without whose genes, sacrifices and forbearance with my misspent youth, I would not have reached my present station from which it was possible to write this story. Honorable mention goes to Bubby.

FORWARD

This family history is being written for my sons Michael and Richard and my grandchildren Joshua, Sean, Sarah, Remington, Madison and their children and their children and so on. In order to impart the true flavor of the story, I was obliged to use some esoteric terms and references. If, by some unlikely chance, others might want to read this chronicle, I apologize for the use thereof and trust they will make allowances. Others will also recognize many similar events in their own families. However, I hope they will appreciate ours nonetheless.

I have changed some names and used only first names to protect the guilty but the events depicted herein, I assure you, are actual. I have also taken the liberty of digressing now and then with extraneous minutiae which seemingly has little to do with the subject at hand. I, howbeit, thought it a good opportunity to pass on some minor history and anecdotes to my progeny. Surely they will not deny me that small perquisite. There are many remembrances that continue to occur to me and will not properly fit into the continuity of events. I have therefore created an additional section at the rear of this thriller in which I have included anecdotes and incidents without regard to relevance.

HISTORICAL BACKGROUND

After years of pogroms (attacks on Jews in Russia) fortune finally smiled on Eastern European Jews in one of those unlikely coincidences of history. Around the year 1880, in the United States, the great western expansion was coming to a close and vast new industries were being born creating the need for massive numbers of workers. This precipitated the adoption of a liberal immigration policy by the government.

Providentially, 1880 saw the breakup of the feudal system in eastern Europe sending some 20,000,000 immigrants to our shores in the ensuing 40 years among whom were 2,000,000 poverty stricken and suffering Jews. To those hapless souls America was the land of milk and honey and the streets are paved with gold. Result of these seemingly unrelated events, both for America and the immigrants, was the unprecedented progress and prosperity that followed.

Were it not for these chance occurrences, I would probably be writing this family history in Russian.

1

During the period from 1889 to 1891 the Eiffel Tower was built, the Sioux Indians were massacred at Wounded Knee, the zipper was patented and Vincent van Gogh committed suicide. Also the first Army-Navy game was played, the Mayo brothers opened their clinic, Queen Victoria ruled England and Czar Alexander III banned all Jews from Moscow and other major cities in Russia.

Oblivious to these events, Yetta (nee Shapiro) and Abraham Wasserman gave birth to a son, Mendel, in the shtetl of Zhitomer near Kiev in the Ukraine. The Wassermans already had a daughter but unfortunately, she would die some years later during childbirth.

Little is known about Abraham's education or occupation but given the plight of the Jews in Russia at that time it would be safe to assume that he was neither an academic nor a virtuoso in the arts. Doubtless, had he been told that all nine of Mendel's grandchildren would earn college degrees (including three lawyers and a doctor), he would no more believe that than he would believe that people would fly through the air like birds during Mendel's lifetime.

There were no public schools of course, so the only formal education Mendel received was in a Chader (Hebrew school), which would prepare him for his Bar Mitzvah. When he left Russia he was fairly fluent in Yiddish and Russian. As a matter of fact, many times when my parents did not want me to know what they were talking about, they would converse in Russian because my mother came over at the age of 9 and in addition to Yiddish she knew some Russian.

My father was a restless young man and there was one little episode that happened in his childhood that might give you a hint as to the kind of boychick he was. He was attending a Chader which was run by a very religious and proper Rabbi. My father had done something wrong(I'm sure) in the classroom and the Rabbi whacked him with a stick. He got so infuriated that he grabbed the Rabbi by his beard (which, of course, every Rabbi had) and held it in a death grip. Nobody could pry his hand loose from the beard. They tried and tried to no avail. Finally, they sent someone to call his father from his workplace and even after his father arrived on the scene, it took a considerable amount of time before they managed to pry his hand loose. Needless to say, he was severely punished with a strap, which was the common punishment for a wayward child in those days. I doubt, however, the Rabbi ever struck him again.

One of the main reasons he left Russia aside from the Pogroms, the golden promise of America and the mass migration that was then in full swing, was the military service law in Russia at the time. It decreed that every young man reaching a certain age must go into the army for two years or more. As often as not, one was kept in the army long after their time of service was at an end. A family would consider themselves lucky if they ever saw their sons again. And going into the Russian army in those days made the Georgia chain gang look like summer camp in the Catskills. Any officer or noncom had full authority to strike you whenever they felt like it, which was quite often. They could curse your mother and do just about anything else they wanted to and you had to take it. The food was terrible, the uniforms were deplorable and it was altogether a miserable existence. And you may be sure, with the rampant anti-semitism existing then, being Jewish just added to the hardship. Russia had millions and millions of people and their strategy in any war, as was shown in World War II, was simply to throw people at the enemy. It didn't matter; life was cheap. So, many young men, when they had the opportunity, fled Russia.

2

Mendel Wasserman, being one of those who fled, arrived in this country at the approximate age of 19 on October 19,1910. Over the years I met a few of his "landsmen"(a person who came from the same town in the old country) and to hear them tell it, no one, aside from his family, was upset over his departure from their neighborhood. He was a tumler (gregarious and spirited person) even at a young age.

Of course, when he came here he was a greenhorn(immigrant). He spoke Yiddish and Russian but here they spoke English and as a greenhorn, he took what jobs he could find. Back in Russia, he had been an apprentice in a barrel factory so he considered himself a cooper (barrel-maker). He got his first job through his cousin, Benny Gross. (The Gross family eventually became quite prominent in Vineland as I understand it.) Benny got him a job with Harry Publicker, a barrel maker who later started Publicker Industries, after the government repealed the prohibition laws in 1933. The company became a giant conglomerate, one of the biggest distillers in the country. However, in those days, he had a small barrel yard. And Harry Publicker, not far removed from greenhorn status himself ran his business like a sweat shop and got a day-and-a-half's work from his workers for a day's pay, as all bosses did in those days. There were no unions or anything close to them. There was no social security or unemployment benefits. Whatever your salary was, you received in cash; a few dollars or so a day and that was it.

My father told me the story that while at work one day, Harry Publicker came over to him and said in Yiddish, "Hey ghreener, go and help load the barrel wagon".

Now when you called somebody "ghreener" (Yiddish colloquialism for greenhorn) it was sort of derogatory amongst the immigrants, who wanted to be assimilated in their new country. My father, being the proud lad that he was, answered in Yiddish as well, "Harry, take this job and shove it up your ass" and walked out. That was the last time he ever had a job.

He started to hang out on a corner (5th & Dickenson Sts, in South Philly). And who else was hanging out at this corner but all the big "knockers"; the number writers, the bootleggers and men of that ilk. Picture a young man in his early twenties and impressionable. He was strong, ambitious and street smart—as smart as they come. He saw these men driving around in Pierce Arrows, Hupmobiles, Reos and Packards (hot cars in those days). They would send him on errands and give him odd jobs here and there. Naturally, as time went on, he decided that he would also become a big shot. So little by little, he started to 'cook' whiskey (vernacular for making moonshine) because it was quite a common practice in those days of the very unpopular Volstead Act (Prohibition).

3

A round this time, the United States entered World War I and the government passed many emergency measures. One of these decreed that if any alien enlisted in the army and agreed to serve for the duration of World War I, they would automatically become a naturalized citizen of the United States. Mendel knew that although he was slowly learning neighborhood street English, his scant knowledge of the language would make it difficult to become naturalized on his own. Not only that, but since it seemed that there was some possible adventure involved and since he wasn't doing too well anyhow, he enlisted on April 30, 1918 in Cleveland, Ohio while visiting a cousin there. When he enlisted, the recruiting Sergeant naturally asked him for his name.

And he replied, "Mendel Wasserman".

The Sergeant asked, "How do you spell it?"

You must understand, of course, that he was just about able to say it, let alone spell it, so he just shrugged. The Sergeant said to my father, "Why don't we shorten and anglicize it? Why don't we make it Morris Weiss?"

My father said, "Fine." And that's how he got his name. He was transferred to Company 'C', 10lst Engineers, Washington, D.C. and on July 5, 1918 Private Morris Weiss became a naturalized citizen of the United States. He was sent to France on July 14, 1918 as part of the American Expeditionary Force after 2½ months of training.

I want to record a couple of war stories he told me. First of all, he didn't understand half the things they were telling him. It was a different kind of war than the one I am familiar with. For one thing, there were lice infested trenches and when they used to fire artillery shells at one another, the shells would explode and leave huge craters like giant

5

fox holes. One day he and an Irish buddy jumped into one of these shell holes for cover, advancing now and then from one crater to another. What happened on that particular day was that they were in this one crater for many hours waiting in vain for their outfit to catch up to them.

After some time the Irishman said," Come on Manny, why don't we try and find our outfit and rejoin them?" (to his army buddies "Manny" was a nickname for Mendel).

They had been sitting in the crater for over 24 hours, through a day and a night. My father replied that until he could see them from where they were he was not moving. The Irishman, having become impatient, said, "Manny, I'm going!"

And as he put his head up above the shelter of the crater a shot rang out. A German sniper had hit him in the eye and as his body fell back into the crater, his eye rolled out of his head. You can be sure that my father didn't budge for another 12 hours until his outfit caught up with him.

Another story was that my father, dashing figure that he was, had met a young French girl and when he walked his post on guard duty she would walk with him now and then to keep him company when it was possible. She would also bring him food that she had prepared and had sneaked into the encampment.

When his outfit neared Paris, he didn't bother with the formality of getting a pass or furlough. Whenever he decided to go to Paris, he simply got on a bus or hitched a ride and went there for a day or two. He was not a very gung-ho soldier although he was in the battles of the Meuse-Argonne and St. Mihiel, two of the major battles of World War I. As a matter of fact I still have the medals he received and the discharge papers citing these fronts.

As a soldier he was not doing very well. He didn't tell me, but given his behavior, I would imagine he spent some time in the company guard house. He was kind of a wild guy and I believe he didn't pay much attention to the rules. So when the armistice was signed and the war was over, his Captain called him in and said, "Weiss, what am I going to do with you?"

And my father, feigning innocence, answered, "What do you mean, sir'?"

"Well, I've been looking over your record and its horrible. My duty dictates that I put you in the guard house for a month or two."

Then the Captain was silent for a few minutes, deep in thought. Finally he said, "I'm married with children and a family at home. I am so happy the war is over and I survived that I am going to be generous with you. I'm going to erase all these violations from your record".

So with a clean slate, our 'tarshid' (intractable male) arrived in the United States for the second time on April 5, 1919. And on April 22, 1919 he was honorably discharged from the U.S. Army at Camp Sherman, Ohio.

4

Now as a 28 year old war veteran and citizen with $60.00 mustering out pay in his pocket he returned to Philadelphia just at the start of the 'roaring twenties'. His cousin Benny Gross, who earlier had helped him get him the job in the barrel factory, now wanted to go into the barrel business with my father. They got themselves two horses and a wagon and became partners. The wagon they bought was one those large, wide-bodied wagons and they started to buy, sell and repair barrels. The only problem was that Benny's wife suddenly became the manager and CEO. It appeared to my father that he was in partnership with Benny's wife and Benny was like a hired hand. At the end of the first week, when it came time to figure out how much money they took in, how much they spent and split up the profits, he was not dealing with Benny but Benny's wife. On top of this, my father had always thought her to be a shrew to begin with. Of course, its easy to guess what happened next. Because of my father's masculine pride and old world machismo, he said to Benny, "Look, either I'm going to be dealing with you as a partner or I want to breakup the partnership."

Needless to say, they broke up the partnership. Given my father's ambition and smarts they could have become very big. One of their contemporaries, a man named Sukonik, started around the same time and did become a big success in the barrel business. Coincidentally, I went to school with one of Sukonik's sons, Marvin many years later.

Soon after they disolved the partnership, my father went out on his own. But just buying and selling barrels was not enough for him, so he started 'cooking' a little whiskey here and there. First, he did it in the basement of a rented store. Then he started to expand and do some decent business. He was a full-fledged bootlegger by this time (the latter half of the "roaring twenties" and early thirties) making good money. This was at a time when the Depression had already started. As a matter of fact, the Depression started for many people in the twenties. It was only the "well heeled" minority who were doing well until the stock market crash in 1929.

He would approach farmers in the outlying counties like Bucks, Montgomery and Delaware as well as New Jersey, most of whom were doing poorly in those days. There were no farm supports from the government. And if they had a bad year, the poor farmers would suffer. It was pretty rough for them as was shown in John Steinbeck's classic "The Grapes of Wrath". It was rough for most people in those days. There were no programs like Social Security, Workman's Compensation or any similar entitlements. You either earned a living or you went without. There was a welfare program referred to as 'Relief' and there were people who applied for it but, unlike today, it was stigmatic to be on relief. It was a "shanda" (disgrace) and embarrassing to be on it. Furthermore, the amount one received could hardly qualify as subsistence. But bad or not, those were the times.

So he contacted these farmers, most of whom were struggling. However, they did have one asset—barns. And he would pay them a monthly rental ($100.00 or so—excellent money in those days) for the use of their barns. He then set up a still and other equipment necessary to make "moonshine". He told them the truth and they didn't care. They were getting enough money to feed their families and that's what counted. He had stills in farms all over the surrounding counties and New Jersey. By the way, some of those farmlands eventually became towns like Jenkintown, Wynnewood, etc. including the Hankin farm (distant relatives of my mother) in what is now the Willow Grove area. We're talking about the late twenties and early thirties. At this point he was doing quite well.

A short episode about my Uncle Murphy (a nickname—his real name was Morris). Uncle Murphy was married to my Aunt Sarah, who was one of my mother's sisters. He was a carpenter and as happened to many Jewish immigrant workingmen in those days (the twenties and thirties) they were being recruited to join the "Communist" party. Their brand of Communism was not the Communism of today but rather a sort of workers' brotherhood with common interests such as working conditions and such. It was, in many ways, the precursor of today's trade unions. They used to attend meetings but they were not political nor did they know what real Communism was. Because he was a workingman, they promised him that his working conditions would improve and he would be much better off by joining these organizations.

Anyway, at one point, Uncle Murphy was laid off, which was common enough in those days when a contractor finished a project. There were no unemployment benefits or Workmen's Compensation programs as we know them today so you just did without when you were laid off. If one was lucky, he would be called back to work when a new project was started. It was common knowledge at this point in time that Mendel was doing well so Aunt Sarah asked her sister Shifra (my mother's Hebrew name) if Mendel could find Murphy a job. This was family so my father gave Murphy a job. He took him out to one of the stills in the country and said, "Look, Murphy, here is a vat containing mash. The mash has to ferment overnight. Once it's fermented, we do this and that and that's how we manufacture moonshine. All you've got to do is watch it. Make sure it doesn't overflow or boil or whatever."

Murphy replied, "OK, Mendel, don't worry about a thing. I'll be here all night and I'll take care of everything".

The next morning, my father arrived at the farm, walked in the door and saw Murphy scooping up buckets full of the mash and throwing it against the wall yelling, "Down with Capitalism! Long live labor!"

With all the alcohol there he must have gotten drunk during the night and went a little wild. Needless to say, that was the end of Uncle Murphy's bootlegging days. Incidentally, I always liked Uncle Murphy and we got along really well. He always had a smile for me and would tell me amusing stories whenever we occasionally met.

5

B eing in the "business", heavy equipment was necessary to accommodate the heavy loads that would have to be transported from place to place. My father would buy an automobile like a Pierce Arrow which was a big heavy car—comparable today, I suppose, to a Cadillac Fleetwood or Lincoln Town Car. And the first thing he would do is drive it from the showroom to a welding shop in South Philly. They would then proceed to remove the rear seats, tear up the rear floorboards and make a trap (hidden compartment) underneath the floor of the rear seat area. They would then put the floor boards and seats back in place. Next, extra-heavy springs were substituted for the original ones. There was good reason for this. In those days they carried the alcohol in five-gallon cans which were quite heavy when full, perhaps 40 or 50 lbs. each. You can imagine how much 8 or 10 fully filled cans would weigh. In an ordinary car the rear of the car would be so depressed when loaded with moonshine that it would be obvious to everyone including the police and hijackers. And with no one sitting in the back seat, it would not take a Phi Beta Kappa to realize that you were hauling a heavy load. Of course, with the extra heavy springs, the car would not look overloaded and most of the time it served its purpose quite well.

A small digression. While we lived on Shunk Street, my father used to buy three or four new cars every year. And each time he would trade, he would get a different color. This was so the cops would not get to know the color of "Mendel's car" and become familiar with it. Tricks of the trade, you know.

Occasionally my father would bring several cans of whiskey into the house and he would allow me help him by letting me pour the whiskey through a funnel stuffed with absorbent cotton into a 5 gallon jug to filter out the impurities that were floating around from the grains. What came through was a clear, white alcohol. Drinkable, but it didn't look like whiskey. So in addition to straining the alcohol, he would send me to the drug store a block away to buy some caramel coloring. For a quarter or so I would bring back a little cough-medicine bottle full of the coloring. He would then pour it into the glass jug, shake it up and Presto! 5 gallons of amber colored moonshine.

There is another episode I remember. During this time, in the early thirties, he went into partnership with an Italian man from Trenton whose name was Pete Pizzaz. This Pete Pizzaz and my father used to bring money into our house every night to be counted. They'd bring canvas bags fill of quarters, dimes, halves, etc. into the dining room. In those days, a half dollar could buy you a whole quart of whiskey, especially moonshine. They would put on the dining room light, draw the shades and start counting the money. They'd have a big pile of silver in the center of the table and my father would let me help. I would pick out all the quarters or dimes, etc. and make piles of coins to be wrapped. They would check the count and then wrap them. Anyway, when they were finished for the night, they would have a whole table full of wrapped coins, you know, hundreds of dollars worth. Then they divided the money.

One day Pete came to my father and in his thick Italian accent, says, "Hey, Mendela! Why should we bother making the moonshine? We have to buy sugar, grain, molasses and all the other supplies for making the whiskey. (They used to buy these supplies from wholesale grocers). Why don't we just wait until another bootlegger has a load and we'll hijack it."

My father, somewhat taken aback, answered, "Wait a minute, Pete. You're talking about strong arm stuff. You have to carry a gun for that kind of thing."

And Pete replies, "Mendela, so what? You don't have all the trouble and expense of making the stuff. You take the whole load and put it in a garage. Then little by little you sell it and that's the easy way to do it."

My father then responded, "Look Pete, I was in the war and they taught me how to handle a gun but I'm not into this kind of thing. I've got a family and I just can't do it. If you want to, we'll split up the partnership. We'll have a reckoning and you can go your way. I wish you the best of luck but I assume that you're not going to hijack any of MY trucks."

So they had a good laugh about it and they split up because Pete was determined to do it his way. This was one of the ways the Mafia began to grow in the Philadelphia area. One year later, they found Pete floating with his face down in the Delaware River, shot behind the head. That was the end of Pete Pizzaz and my father's connections with that group. However, being in the business my father was in, he would, on occasion, meet members of the Jewish mafia. As a matter of fact, he became very good friends with Willie who was a top lieutenant in the Philadelphia area. Everyone knew that Mendel, although in the rackets, was not a strong arm type. More about Willie later on.

6

I want to go back in time a bit and tell you now what I know about the courtship of my mother. I'll get back to the bootlegging days further on. My mother's sister Lily was married to Harry Forbes, a New Yorker. He introduced Mendel to Sylvie and they started to 'date'. In those days they would go to the silent movies or Levis' at 6th and Lombard Sts. known for their famous hot dogs, fish cakes and champagne sodas. My mother told me that there was another man, a laundryman, who was courting her at the same time. Of course, my mother's family was somewhat less than overjoyed when they found out the business my father was in, which was, of course, bootlegging. Especially my grandmother! The family on my mother's side were straight legitimate people and they trembled at the thought. (By the way, I had a similar experience when I was courting Rina. When her Uncle Nat told Edith and Harry Rosen (her parents) that Mendel was a gambler and ex bootlegger, they wanted Rina to stop seeing me,)

The family reasoned, however, that since my mother was seeing another man, the situation was not hopeless. The other man was making a legitimate living. He was in the laundry business and had started to supply linens to institutions like hospitals, restaurants and so on. He was a decent looking man and an all around nice guy. Although she was seriously considering him, what turned her off, was a habit he had of taking his tie and curling it, i.e., rolling it up then letting it out again. Rolling it up and letting it down. He was probably shy and a bit nervous but it used to drive her crazy, his rolling the tie up and down. And believe it or not, to hear her tell it, that was one of the reasons she gave up on him. I would have to guess, however, that the main reason was that she had fallen for Mendel. She once confessed to me that she was struck by Mendel's dapper, dashing style. Incidentally, the man

17

later became very successful and the business he started still exists today. They supply restaurants, hotels, etc. with laundry and linen service.

Sylvia Chirlin and Mendel Weiss were married May 3, 1923 by Rabbi Moses Lipschitz. I was born February 23, 1924 (they didn't waste any time in those days) at 3:30 in the morning at 2430 S. American Street in So. Phila. during a raging snowstorm—so mother told me. We then moved to West Philly for a short time and then to Eighth and Porter Sts. in South Phila. again. We lived on the east side of Eight St. between Porter and Ritner until I was about three years old. (I am being specific in the event that one of my progeny might someday want to make a pilgrimage to these sacred sites. I understand that 2430 S. American St. is already being considered a National Historic Site.)

While we were living on Eighth St. I remember my father bought me a model car, you know, these small cars in which you use foot peddles to make them go. He brought it back from the store with the help of Davie Glass, a man who used to work for him and as it turned out, became like a second father to me. (Davie will appear later in this tale). They took it out of the truck and put it on the sidewalk. Then Mendel said, "Eshiala (the diminutive familiar for my Hebrew name Eshia) here is a present for you".

I can remember only a few other times in my life when I was so ecstatic. Everyone knew that I was in love with automobiles as a child so it was like giving me the moon. It was unbelievable. You know, one of those fancy cars with a horn, windshield, etc. It made such an impression on me that I will always remember these details.

Around this time they were building new houses on Shunk Street near Fifth. In those days many people couldn't afford to buy a house so they rented. I must mention that while we were living on Eighth Street, my grandmother and my youngest aunt, i.e., my mother's youngest sister, Minnie, who never married, lived with us. My mother at this time became pregnant with Shirley Ruth and when they found out about the new houses being built at Fifth and Shunk we moved to

440 Shunk Street. So it was my grandmother, Aunt Minnie, my mother, my father, me and then Shirley—all living in a house with 3 small bedrooms and 1 bath. (Quite common in those days)

My father was doing well then and he started to expand in the bootlegging business. He would have been "backing numbers" (similar to today's state sponsored lottery which was illegal then) but he didn't know how to read or write English very well at that time. He eventually started taking English lessons later on in the 30's. A private tutor used to come to the house to teach him. He eventually learned how to read fairly well and was able to print but never was able to write in longhand.

7

At this point in time (the 1930s) we were all living on Shunk Street and Mendel was doing quite well. We were one of the well-off families in the neighborhood and I was always dressed like little Lord Fauntleroy. When we'd come down to Atlantic City for the summer, we didn't stay in an apartment like most. We went to a hotel where they had elevators and served every meal. The mention of Atlantic City reminds me of another little anecdote.

One summer when I was about 2½ years old my father used to delight in taking me to the beach because on the long blocks uptown there were hundreds of cars parked in a row. As I mentioned previously, I had established a love affair with automobiles ever since my father bought me that toy car in South Philly on Eighth St. I was able to name just about every brand of auto of that period. This prompted my father to show off my talent to his friends at every opportunity. As we would walk to the beach, he would say, "What kind of car is that, Eshiala?"

I would reply, "That's a "Fordel or a Chevrolayka". I was able to name every brand of car in those days such as the Pierce Arrow, Hupmobile, etc. What made it special was my age; what made it hysterically funny was my Yiddish accent. At the time, I knew very little English.

I want to mention an episode where I learned a bit about public relations. My father had a small semi trailer in which he used to haul raw materials. Being street smart, he soon realized that envy and jealousy were common human emotions so he decided on a good neighbor policy. One of his stills was located near a shoe factory somewhere in upstate Pennsylvania. This factory, in the course of its manufacturing, would wind up with odds and ends. By that I mean that they would find a left shoe with damage on it and throw it into a pile. Another time it would be a right shoe. The black didn't come out properly or the black dye had smeared on the white and so on. Eventually they wound up with a giant pile of mismatched shoes, rejects and seconds.

One day my father took the trailer and went up to the factory with a couple of his men. He made a deal with the owner and wound up with the whole pile of shoes for a pittance. They were glad to get rid of them. He loaded up the trailer with the shoes, came back to Fifth and Shunk and parked it in front of our house. Then he sent me around the neighborhood to knock on everybody's door to tell them to come and get free shoes. All they had to do was pick them out. Remember, this is during the depression, the thirties, when people hardly had enough to eat.

So I told the neighbors and they started to pick out shoes. Left-handed shoes, right-handed shoes, even high button shoes. I remember the neighbors having a great time; laughing and joking and throwing shoes at one another in an effort to make a match. But everybody went home with shoes. And what was left over they finally dumped on the city dump which was in back of our house. This gesture established Mendel as a good neighbor with a reputation as 'standup guy' in South Philly when word got around.

Another PR exercise he would do. He had another cousin, one Benny Shapiro, who lived in Salem, New Jersey near the bay. Every year just before Passover when people would need fish for the holiday gefilte fish, he would rent a small tank trailer and hook it to the rear of his car. Then he'd go down to the bay area near Salem and load up with live carp. He'd bring it back, park it in front of the house and send me out to get the neighbors again. I would tell them to come and get free fish for yuntiff (holiday). The fish were alive and fresh, still swimming around in the tank; a condition that was and still is so important to many finicky Jewish housewives.

I just remembered another little episode about the Depression days. At home, we would eat strawberries with sour cream. One day I was visiting with one of my friends in his house on Fifth Street and I saw him and his brother eating strawberries. But instead of covering them with sour cream, they used milk. In my naiveté, I said, "How can you eat strawberries with milk? You're supposed to use sour cream."

Of course, they didn't want to say that they couldn't afford sour cream which was more expensive, and I, naive as I was, didn't realize it. Only days later, when I mentioned the incident to my mother, did I come to know the reason they used milk instead of sour cream.

Anyway, things were going along nicely for awhile and my mother had become pregnant again. I was 12 years old at this time and it was summertime, August 17, 1936 to be exact. I was playing in a nearby driveway where Bubby found me and said, "Eshiala, your mother just had a baby boy."

"That's nice, Bubby", I replied and kept on playing with my friends. As a 12 year old, I was somewhat less than overwhelmed at the news. That afternoon around 5 o'clock as I came off the street for dinner my Aunt Minnie said to me, "Harold, did you know your mother had a little girl today?"

They were afraid to tell me that my mother had twins and give them a "kinanhura" (sort of a jinx). They were afraid that God would figure it was too much of a blessing and he would take it away for some reason. Later, my father came home and told me that I have another sister and a brother.

I said, "What are you talking about?' And I told him what Bubby and Aunt Minnie had told me.

He said,"No! No! Your mother had twins. A boy and a girl and they're both" roitas" (redheads) like your mother. "Mendel was not a very superstitious man. And so there came upon the land Alvin Milton and eighteen minutes later Elaine Marcia.

By coincidence, on August 17, 1936, a man named John Avena, who was the head of the Philadelphia/New Jersey Mafia, came out of a building on Washington Avenue in South Philly with one of our neighbors, Marty Feldstein, a numbers banker. What they were doing together is unknown but I guess they had had a business meeting. As they walked out of this building near the Ninth Street Italian market, one of those big convertible sedans like you see in the movies, came by with machine guns blazing and killed them both. Rumor had it that they had been after Avena and it was Feldstein's bad luck to be with him. The Feldsteins lived three houses away from us and one son, Howard, was one of my lifelong friends. My grandmother, being as superstitious as she was, said, "See, this is how God runs the world. Two people died and two others replaced them today." Of course she was referring to the twins and at the time we believed it.

8

F LASHBACK! It is 1933 and the United States Congress passed the 21st Amendment which repealed the 18th Ammendment that prohibited the sale, use, possession or manufacture of alcohol (commonly known as the Volstead Act). Mendel was riding high but he decided to "go legitimate"(a popular phrase in those days).

Two blocks from where we lived, on the NW corner of 7th and Shunk Streets he bought the property and opened a bar and restaurant. He spared no expense and Mendel's place became the talk of the town. The restaurant was next door to a butcher shop which made it convenient because the restaurant specialized in steaks and chops. A cousin, who was a cabinetmaker, built him a magnificent mahogany bar and steam table—cafeteria style. Halfway along the length of the bar was a break in the continuity. It was designed this way so that a waitress could go from the back of the bar and serve the patrons seated in booths across the aisle from the bar without having to go all the way to the end of it. Don't get bored with these details because they will become significant in a moment.

He had a grand opening and it was a huge success. All the wise guys, number writers and "big shots" came down to Mendel's place to have a steak and hang out. It was the Dave Shore's and Lew Tendler's of South Philly and doing quite well. My mother worked there part time to help out with the food preparation and look after things if my father had to go out. I was around 9 years old and I used to like to hang out there whenever I could. My grandmother would baby-sit with Shirley who was only 6 at the time.

One fateful day two guys came in to have dinner. Harry Comers and Spiegel, both number writers, sat down facing each other in a booth directly across from the aforementioned break in the bar. For an appetizer they ordered chopped cow's brains with chicken fat and chopped onions. This was a very popular delicacy in those days (pre-cholesterol) and still is in some places. I used to love it and ate it all the time. As an entree they ordered steaks. However the cook told my father that they had run out of steaks, so my father went next door to the butcher shop to buy more.

While Mendel is in the butcher shop, they're sitting and eating and talking with my mother who was standing across the aisle in the break of the bar, a distance of about five feet. In walks another habitué named William Slatko alias Slats. He was known around town as a wise guy and tough guy—that sort of thing. Speigel was sitting with his back toward the entrance door and doesn't see Slats walk in. Slats is carrying a gun and shoots Spiegel in the back of his head behind the ear and as Speigel slumps forward, his brains, ironically, run into the plate of cow brains that he was eating. Slats kept right on walking through the kitchen, out the back door and through an alley to Porter Street where he left the gun in an empty milk bottle. And he's gone!

All this, right in front of Harry Comers and my mother. My mother, as you will remember, was directly across the aisle from the booth they were sitting in. By the way, my aunt Minnie who was as innocent and naïve as an adult could be, was standing in the kitchen when Slats came running through. Fortunately, my mother had the presence of mind to push her out the back door and send her home before the police arrived. Nobody ever found out.

ASIDE. A couple of weeks before this, Slats had gone into the men's room and being friendly with all the guys that used to hang out there, I locked him in as a practical joke. At the age of nine, I thought it was cute but he was furious. He rammed the door open, grabbed my arm and started to twist it. Fortunately, my father walked in and told Slats to release me. Everyone knew my father was connected so they usually did what he said. In addition, it was his place and I guess Slats realized I was only a kid, so he let me go.

Now, back to the story. Needless to say, the place became a bedlam; a scene from NYPD Blue. Squad cars with lights flashing, dozens of police, etc. Of course, the Homicide Squad took over and started questioning everyone. Why was my mother standing across from them? Why did Mendel go to the butcher shop at that particular time? Was that a signal to Slats to come in and do Spiegel? The homicide detectives refused to believe that my father wasn't connected somehow with the homicide. They figured, you know, with his background and all, that he could have gone out to get the steaks as a signal for Slats to come in to kill Spiegel. So they questioned Comers, the cook and everyone who was anywhere near the place at the time. Afterward, my father figured that Slats was waiting outside and when he saw him go next door to the butcher shop he seized the opportunity and executed his nefarious plan. By the way, it was a known fact that Slats was a drug user and was surely under the influence that night.

The result of this incident was that a business that had such great promise, simply died soon afterward. People were afraid to come into the place. Within six months my father just abandoned it. He always liked the restaurant business so he soon opened the Russian Kretchma (Russian for nightclub) on the south side of Locust Street just west of Broad in center city. He fashioned it after a cabaret he had seen in New York. It was a great place as I remember—Russian motif and decor inside with a doorman dressed as a Cossack outside. But the moment had passed. Nightclubs and bars such as Jack Lynch's Walton Roof, Benny the Bum's Restaurant and the like were opening all over. I have to imagine that the competition became fierce and I think within a year or so the Kretchma was no more. He did open another steak house at 9th and Spruce but it too only lasted a short time.

Justice will be done! William Slatko was apprehended within a year and of course, everyone connected with the crime was subpoenaed to testify at the trial. During the trial, the District Attorney stationed a police officer on our porch around the clock to make sure no one approached my mother. Harry Comers, being a gambler and not wanting to get involved any further, said he couldn't remember the incident exactly and could not positively identify Slats as the perpetrator. My mother, on the other hand, could remember everything. When she took the witness stand the District Attorney said, "Mrs. Weiss, please look around this courtroom. Do you see the person who shot Mr. Spiegel?"

Without a moment's hesitation and without blinking an eye she pointed to Slats and said, "That's him!"

The jury, supplied with an eyewitness to the murder, quickly found him guilty and the judge sentenced William Slatko to life imprisonment. My mother had a vendetta for Slats and was especially bitter at him because of what he had done. She and her husband had been making a comfortable legitimate living and by choosing her place to commit murder he ruined the business. Over the years she would ask me rhetorically, "If he had to kill Spiegel why couldn't he have picked somewhere else to do it?"

As to the suspicion by the police that my father had somehow been involved, I guess they finally figured out that if my father was in on it, he wouldn't have done it in a way that would ruin his own business. End of story? No way!

9

E pilogue to murder. It was now after World War II. Everyone had long forgotten about Slats. My father was making a decent living in a teahouse of which I shall subsequently speak. The family had, by then, moved to 2410 S. Third Street because before the war, the land-lord on Shunk Street had wanted to raise the rent from $30.00 a month.

My father's best friend and a former employee in the bootlegging days had moved to Miami Beach in 1938. As I mentioned previously, his name was Davie Glass and I shall speak of him at length later on. He came up from Florida with the sole purpose of talking to my father about Slats. By this time, Slats had been in jail around 13 years or so but he must have had an important friend somewhere in Las Vegas to have been able to devise the following scheme.

They would buy off a judge who would then allow witnesses in the case to change their testimony. And who was the key witness, you might ask. That's right, our very own Sylvia Weiss. The judge was already lined up and it was only a question of how much. Now they had to get to Sylvia Weiss. And how does one accomplish that? She's legitimate and straight as an arrow. When there's a legitimate person involved, most often it was "hands off" by the wise guys. How can they approach her to get her to change her testimony? They accurately reached the conclusion that they had to go through Mendel. And how do you get to Mendel? Davie Glass was the man because it was common knowledge that they were the closest of friends most of their lives. So they contacted Davie and asked him to go up and present Mendel with the proposition.

Davie came up from Florida especially to meet with my father and said, "Mendel, there are certain people who are interested in getting Slats out of jail. This is the way they want to do it."

He then proceeds to tell him how the judge will be fixed. Then, at a certain time and place a hearing will be held to open the case again and all Sylvie (familiar name used by people close to my mother) had to say was, "I've thought about my testimony all these years and the more I thought about it, the more I am just not sure anymore that William Slatko was the man who shot Mr. Spiegel."

For this, they offered her $10,000.00 (a virtual fortune in those days) and had she been so inclined, she could have negotiated for more. Just about whatever she wanted for a few minutes of her time with no risk.

My father replied, "Davie, I know Sylvie and it would be like talking to a wall. But since you've gone to this much trouble, I'll talk to her."

My father came home and told my mother the story—anything you want, etc. My mother's reply was as quick as it was predictable and in Yiddish says, "Let him burn in hell. I should let that murderer go? Absolutely not!"

My father didn't say another word, went back to Davie and told him what my mother had said. Davie went back to Florida, relayed the message (not, perhaps, in the same terms) and they never bothered my mother again.

To finish the Slats saga. He eventually got out in the early fifties, after spending about 15 years in jail. When he got out he went to Vegas and got a job there. He died soon after from poor health. To me, the most fascinating aspect of the whole affair was the experience my mother went through, i.e., being a witness to an actual murder not more than six feet away. And her being such a straight arrow. Not many people have ever been through anything like that.

10

Time marches on! The twins had arrived and it was time for my Bar Mitzvah. But before I go into that and beyond, I want to bring my mother's story up to this point. Shifra Chirlin was born in 1902 in the shtetl of Mogilev, Belo-Russia which is located about 200 miles east of Minsk. She was next to the youngest of ten children born to Rose and Eshia Chirlin. Rose's father, one Nachem Getzanek, was, for those days, a rather prosperous butcher who had several cows and other things of value. He was six feet tall, handsome as a movie star and every bit the pious and stately patriarch. His wife and he were, however, unable to conceive at one point and were told by the rabbi to perform a 'mitzvah' (good deed which would earn a blessing from God).

He had 'adopted' an orphan and he would frequently invite this poor Yeshiva student for Sabbath dinner (Friday night) which was considered a mitzvah as well. He also made weddings for some of the poorer girls in town. Miracle of miracles, they eventually had 3 daughters—Mima, Bubby and one other, all three of whom lived to be in their 80's.

He was prosperous enough to send his daughter Rose to Hebrew school which was quite rare for a girl. Nachem was a Kohen (High Priest) and lived to be 88. (By the way, Mendel held himself out to be a Kohen also, but knowing his devilish ways, I believe he did this to avoid certain unpleasantness like viewing dead bodies at funerals which was one of the perks of a Kohen.)

Unfortunately, Nachem did not make a match for his daughter that in any way resembled himself. The groom, Eshia, was a blacksmith and was chosen for Rose but never amounted to much with one exception. In the area of procreation, he was a prolific legend in his own time. And for some reason, each time Rose became pregnant, which, as you realize, was almost her perennial condition, she went back to her father's house for the duration. As was common in those days, however, two of Rose's children died in infancy.

Eshia Chirlin passed away when Shifra was 5 years old in 1907 (probably from an overworked libido or prostate) and it was soon decided that the family would migrate to America as some of Rose's family had already done. She had 11 siblings, all but 2 of whom beside herself died early. Of course, Rose had nowhere near enough money to pay the travel costs of her and her eight children, so as was widely practiced in those days, Jacob, Meyer and Elizabeth came over first. They were brought over by their cousins, Sam Lankin and Mary Hankin who were already here. (I must interrupt the story to explain the confusion regarding the family names. I doubt that anyone knows the original name but due to the turmoil of the migration and lack of education at that time, our family name(s) were recorded variously as Cherlin, Chirlin, Serlin and Sirlin and cousins Hankin and Lankin. So if you come across anyone with these names, treat them like family since they probably are.)

To go on. They got jobs here, the boys as carpenters, Elizabeth as a seamstress and they saved enough money eventually to send for my grandmother Rose and her daughters Sarah, Lillian, Sylvia, Minnie and son Michel.

They traveled by rail (lst class of course) across Poland to Bremen, Germany where they were to board the ship to America. In Bremen, the son Michel was refused permission to come to America because of an eye disease and had to go back to Russia where he remained the rest of his life. One can only imagine the grief that befell my grandmother when she had to make the decision of going on without her son.

If that isn't enough to break your heart, the following story might just do it. While sitting on a bench in the station, waiting to be boarded, Rose was approached by an elderly Jewish woman who engaged her in seemingly innocent conversation. In Yiddish, they talked about their home towns, where they are going and so on. She then suggested to Rose that they take a short walk as it will be awhile until they have to board. Leaving Sarah to watch the others, Rose and her new friend started to walk through the terminal. Suddenly a man comes running up to them, overwrought and raving that someone had stolen his billfold along with the money that was in it. The woman, to show her innocence, took out her money, gives it to the man who then inspects it and returns it to her saying that it wasn't his. He then asked to see Rose's money and Rose, who had never been more than 10 miles from home in her entire life, reached into her bosom and hands him her entire stake of $50.00. He seemingly checked it over and saying it wasn't his money either, returns the bundle to Rose and takes off. The woman then said goodbye to Rose and departed also. Rose returned to her daughters and before she put the money away she discovered that the money had turned to cut-up newspaper.

The result of this little episode was that she and her daughters had to remain in Bremen for three additional weeks until her sons in the States could send her more. The sons had to borrow the new $50.00 from a worker's club (mistakenly called a 'corporation' in those days) which took them a year of weekly installments to repay. Family was everything then. The agency who handled the trip was able to find them a place to sleep and provided them with food (pea soup and pea-nut butter sandwiches) while they waited.

Finally, after a glorious crossing in a penthouse suite aboard the SS Dominion, Rose Chirlin and her daughters disembarked in the port of Philadelphia on September 12, 1911. The younger daughters were soon enrolled in school, but I do not know which of them went and for how long. The older ones got jobs in a cigar factory and life went on like that until they each married (with the exception of the youngest, Minnie).

As to my mother Sylvia, there is not a lot to tell regarding her life here until she married and as I have already related, she played a signif-icant role in events subsequent to that time.

Now to Eshiala's Bar Mitzvah. Mendel was doing pretty good in 1937 so he rented Stanton Hall at Moyamensing and Snyder Avenues and made a Bar Mitzvah banquet to end them all. It cost the unheard of sum of $500.00 at a time when a man earning $25.00 per week was able to support a family and our monthly rent for a 3 bedroom house on Shunk St. was $30.00. I had 'ushers' who carried electrically lit Torahs and walked down the aisle, two at a time and formed sort of an honor guard through which I finally marched up to the stage. My friends (Lou included) and some cousins were the ushers. Louie, of course, could not let things go by without some mischief, so he smeared a whole square of ice cream over the front of my cousin Jackie Chirlin's suit.

I then gave a speech in Yiddish and since there were a couple of tables full of my father's Italian 'business associates', I repeated it in English for their benefit. My speech began, "Dear friends, beloved relatives and respected elders. Today I am a man. It is my 13th birthday and I want to thank my parents, etc, etc." It was an affair to remember.

11

The glow of my beautiful Bar Mitzvah did not last long. Mendel was, I suppose, at the zenith of his bootlegging career at this time. He had 7 or 8 employees and I remember the names of a few : Davie Glass, Benny Katz, Jackie Myers and Hymie Yeslow. Soon after the affair, Yeslow was arrested by federal alcohol agents and the first thing he did was offer them the name of the boss, Mendel Weiss. He identified the locations of all the stills and what other details they needed to make a case against Mendel who was subsequently arrested, charged and brought to trial. I still remember the judge's name—U.S. District Court Judge Maris.

My father, of course, tried to reach the judge through various 'big time' connections in Washington, Philadelphia and New York and retained the best trial lawyer in the area. All this maneuvering cost him his fortune and was only successful to the extent that he received a suspended sentence and was fined $10,000.00 (approximately $150,000.in today's money) and put on probation. He was thus drained financially. By the way, Yeslow, ironically, suffered the same fate and was known from then on as the Rat. He moved to Florida and was never heard from again.

As it turned out there was one positive aspect to these events and that was that it happened during the summer months when I was not in school. This enabled me to get a job. I had two uncles named Meyer; Meyer (Pete) Chirlin, my mother's brother and Meyer Prager, who had married my mother's sister Elizabeth (Laika). Meyer Prager (I taught him how to drive years later) owned, with his family, the largest newsstand in the city of Philadelphia on the NW corner of 13th and Market streets. It was opened 24 hours a day, 365 days a year. It offered newspapers and magazines from every major city in the country and some parts of the world. It was quite famous throughout the area. They augmented this business with a homemade tip sheet on the horse races at the various tracks outside of Pennsylvania. Racetracks were not yet legal in Pennsylvania.

Anyway, Uncle Meyer Prager gave me a job at the newsstand for the summer recognizing, of course, how badly we needed the money. This was 1939 and I was paid the princely sum of $12.50 per week which was fair under the circumstances. It was, however, pretty brutal work even for a big strapping 15 year old like myself.

Let me explain. At the time there were three evening newspapers ; the Daily News, the Evening Bulletin and the Evening Ledger. There were, as well, two morning papers; the Record and the Inquirer. The printing plants of these newspapers were within a two or three block radius of the stand. Each of these papers had several editions; the Bulletin even had a five star final. In part, my job was to go to the various paper locations and bring back a load of the latest editions. A load consisted of 100 newspapers wrapped with wire. And I would schlep them on my shoulders in the 'center city' heat and humidity of mid-summer. Then I'd go back an hour later and get the next edition.

In addition, I walked to 15th and Market streets to pick up the out of town newspapers that came in on the trains. A bit of history here. There were tracks from the 30th Street Railroad Station that ran along Market Street to 15th Street and terminated there right in the center of town. The tracks had been laid on an elevated viaduct about 30 feet above the street level and came to be known as the Chinese Wall (it really resembled it). It was there at 15th Street that I would pick up the foreign and out of town publications. I have to confess that I have no happy memories of that summer but I remain grateful to my Uncle Meyer for having let me work there. Aside from a pittance my mother received from the Veteran's Administration I was, at 15, the only other support of the family. I should say, however, that I suspect my mother's sisters, whosoever's husband was making a decent living, did, from time to time, give her some monetary help.

To go on. I would come home and give my mother the $12.50. There were no payroll taxes in those days, at least not for me. At this time, there was my mother, my three siblings and me to support. My Aunt Minnie was just about able to provide for herself and my grandmother who were living with us. And as you can guess, none of us were living in the lap of luxury. When my mother saw how hard I was working, unbeknownst to anyone else in the family, she would slip me a half dollar spending money in addition to what I needed for trolley fare and lunches. This was $.50 cents for the week. Regardless of what the times were like, this was not big bucks by any stretch of the imagination. Could this possibly explain my Depression mentality?

12

Summer finally passed and my father was financially broke of course, but worse than that I believe the experience took a lot out of him psychologically. Through an old friend he got a job with a refrigeration company as a salesman. It was a nominal job because he had to show the authorities that he had gainful employment.

If he didn't have enough problems at that time, he suffered a heart attack that very winter. Being a veteran he insisted on going to the Naval Hospital in League Island Park near the Philadelphia Navy Yard. He had just bought an old junker of a car which was all he could afford. It was mid-winter and it was snowing and raining most of the time. My mother had no way of getting to the hospital so at the age of 15 without a driver's license I drove her to the Naval Hospital, waited for her because I wasn't allowed in the hospital, and then drove her back. One can imagine how desperate she was, being more law abiding than Mother Teresa, to allow me to drive the car without a license.

Before I continue I want to say something more about the character of Mendel Weiss. Although he was in the "rackets",i.e., the numbers business, gambling, bootlegging and things like that, when he came home for dinner in the evening it was like he had walked through a magic doorway. He was an absolutely devoted and ideal father. He disciplined the children, saw to the family's needs, etc.

I remember at Christmas time being envious when all the Gentile kids would get gifts, Shirley and I would hang up our stockings on the stair banister (we had no fireplace, of course) and he would fill them with coal from the cellar. But then he and Sylvia would go to Cherry's on Market Street, which was the biggest and most famous candy store in 'center city'. You can imagine Shirley's and my delight when the next morning there would be all kinds of fancy chocolates and candies overflowing from the stockings. He was a real "mench" and I was nuts about him as were most of the people who knew him. When I was building the house at the shore, I met the mother-in-law of Dr. Henry Greenwood, a neighbor. As it turned out, Marcia Greenwood and her mother once lived at 5th St. and Oregon Avenue in South Philly exactly one block away from us. We started to reminisce and when I told her that I was Mendel Weiss' son, she started to cry like a baby and I was the Greenwoods' favorite from then on.

When my father died I was a grown man, married with a child and another on the way. It was about two months before Michael was born. I completely adored him and broke out in a rash between my legs that lasted almost six months. It itched so badly that when I was out in company, I'd have to go to the men's room, drop my pants and scratch. From the scratching, I developed huge welts. The doctor diagnosed the itching as a psychological reaction to his death.

Back to the story. When my father came out of the hospital he started to look around for something to do. His options were limited due to a lack of formal education among other things. So he stayed with the areas that he knew best. Gambling, whiskey and food.

He rented a small store at 640 W. Moyamensing Avenue in South Philly and opened a 'Russian Tea Room'(he eventually bought the property which was no big deal even in its best days). He outfitted the store with used tables and chairs. In the rear there was a pint-sized kitchen and in the front he had a small counter. Underneath the counter he had bottles of whiskey which he would sell by the drink (without a liquor license of course) along with various foods my mother would prepare at home. His customers consisted mainly of Jewish workingmen such as carpenters, plumbers, masons, owners of 'mom and pop' stores on 7th Street which was the Jewish version of the Italian market on 9th Street. Most of them were immigrants like himself and on their days off they would hang out at the 'tea room'. He would rent the tables to them by the hour and provide the cards so that they could play cards—mostly pinochle. You may assume, with such a gathering, there was no shortage of kibitzers looking over the players' shoulders and offering them 'expert' advice. It was what one could call a poor man's social club.

On weekends, my mother would make pastrami fish, stuffed kishka (derma) and/or other ethnic delicacies which were always loaded with lots of garlic and hot spices. Mendel would go to the store on Sunday mornings with all these pots full of food which he would sell at the front counter along with the whiskey. On Sundays, the legitimate bars were closed in Pennsylvania so he was quite busy on that day. It was generally known in South Philly that if you wanted a shot or a beer or both you could always get it at Mendel's place. As a matter of fact many an off duty policeman would drop in for a drink and some pinochle. Of course, the cops from the precinct captain on down were on the payroll and permitted this to go on because they knew it was no big mafia operation and simply provided a place for these senior citizens to hang out and enjoy themselves.

As was bound to happen occasionally, some yenta would come storming in to look for her missing husband and on finding him, almost literally drag him home to the amusement and laughter of the others. I recall one incident when this man, Schmerel the balagula (moving man), came in, ate a piece of salty herring and a piece of garlic and called out to Mendel for a double double Calvert Reserve. Not a double shot, mind you, but a double double shot. It was a water glass full of liquor. He emptied the glass in a gulp and sat down to play cards until his wife came from two blocks away and literally pulled him out of the store. Just like in the movies. But it was a hangout for these men where they could be with their friends and pass some time. Besides, they had no place else to go.

And so he made a decent living. But gambling was in his blood and he would make most of his money gambling himself. First of all he was a world class pinochle player. After the first few cards were played, he just about knew what everybody had in their hands. He was not only a real pro at pinochle but he was an expert klabiotch player as well. Klabiotch is an old eastern European game that is played with the cards from the 7 to the Ace. I watched them play for years and still could not understand the game. It seemed to me that at one point a 7 beat a 5 and at other times it seemed that a 5 took a 7. I never did figure it out. But it's a real gambler's game and when my father found someone who knew the game he made a decent day's pay.

There was one man, known to one and all as Glider or 'Old Man Glider' if you wanted to be sure you had the right Glider. He owned a restaurant around the corner on Seventh and Wolf and fancied himself a superb pinochle player. Old Man Glider helped support my father for many years because my father would allow himself to be sucked into a game and after letting Glider win a little, he would make himself a week's pay in a couple of hours. It was like taking candy from a baby.

13

Things went along quietly like this for a while until Pearl Harbor. Many of the skilled workers who were Mendel's customers were suddenly in demand because of the need for their skills in the war effort. Carpenters, electricians, metal workers, etc. most of whom could only find work 2 or 3 days a week suddenly got jobs in defense industries at 3 and 4 times the pay they were earning previously. And they could work as many as 7 days a week if they desired at 'time and a half'. At first, this situation had an adverse effect on the tea room in that the customers no longer had the time to hang around and 'party'. However, the fickle finger of fate can, on occasion, be beneficial. While they did not have much time to spend at Mendel's place, their pockets were bulging as they never did before. It did not take very long for my father, given his enterprising spirit, to figure out a solution to this turn of events.

Every Friday night, when, by coincidence, his customers had their fresh salary in hand, he would run an all night poker game in one of the upstairs bedrooms atop the teahouse. It would start around 9 PM and end at 6 AM Saturday. He would deal the entire night except for 'relief breaks' and he would cut 25 cents (frequently 50 or 75) from each pot for the house. It may not seem like much, but believe me, after 8 or 9 hours he was often the only winner. For those of you who are familiar with the game, the stakes were $.25, $.50 and $1.00. which in those days (when a brand new Chevrolet Coupe cost $750.00) made for an interesting evening. Of course, as usually happens, the stakes were raised during the last hour. The games went on all through the war and for some time afterward. By then he had replenished his 'nest egg' to the extent that he was able to buy a home for cash in the 'Northeast'. Needless to say, the local gendarmes also benefited from the action. Every time I reminisce about those Friday nights, I can't help but think of Nathan Detroit's oldest established permanent floating crap game from "Guys and Dolls".

14

Never a dull moment. In 1952 Mendel Weiss received a notice from the Internal Revenue Service that he was going to be audited. This was a result of a crackdown by the Internal Revenue Service on all known 'racket guys' at that time. They used what is known as the 'net worth' method of determining a taxpayer's tax liability. This means that if the increase of one's assets from the beginning of a year to the end of that year materially exceeds their reported income, that difference is considered additional taxable income. By this time, we had already moved to the new house on Unruh Street and I suspect it was one of the reasons my father's name was chosen for an audit. The house cost the princely sum of $12,500. In those days, it was decent money and dad paid for it in cash. Do I have to tell you that he had kept no books or records? Everything he ever did was in cash. So Jack Felzer, a crackerjack accountant for whom I was then working and from whom I learned a tremendous amount, accompanied us to the audit as Mendel's representative.

The revenue agent was very stern and was licking his chops in anticipation of nailing a big time racketeer. How was he to know that he would be dealing with such a perspicacious pirate. I have to laugh when I recall the story. To everyone's surprise including Felzer's, my father produced a bound copybook, like kids use in school. And in it, written in Yiddish, was herring—$1.26, bread—$.65 and so on. He tells the agent that he could not read nor write English and that he did the best he could. The IRS examiner says, "What's this?"

Daddy answers, "These are my books".

To which the already reddening agent asks, "Where are your real books?"

"These are my real books. I don't know any other way to write."

Frustrated, the agent, whose voice was rapidly reaching an ever higher pitch, declared, "How can I perform an audit on these records?"

An exemplar of innocence, Mendel replied, "Point to any item you want to know about and I'll translate it for you".

By now, Jack and I were bursting at the seams with restrained laughter and the agent is just bursting. He finally came to the conclusion that his case was not very strong. If this man doesn't know the English language, what is one to do? So he reluctantly realized that he was wasting his time with this small fry, settled for $100.00 and wiped the slate clean.

Mendel was always shrewd and calculating but never without impish and comedic overtones and never malicious. A brief anecdote comes to mind that illustrates my characterization of him. One afternoon he needed to get a shave and a haircut so naturally he went to Moishe the barber on McKean St. just east of 7$^{th.}$ The shop was packed with steady customers, it being close to a holiday. Among those waiting was an old friend, Jake Goldstein, founder of Goldstein's Funeral Parlor. Mendel, with a somber and serious expression on his face, greeted him with, "Hello, Jake. My mother-in-law passed away. Would you mind giving me your turn?"

Without a second's hesitation, Jake answered, "Of course not".

Whereupon Mendel gets into the barber's chair. Moishe gives him the shave and haircut and as he steps off the chair, Jake, probably in the hope of getting the funeral business asked, "When did she die?"

With an impish grin, Mendel answers, "About 4 years ago".

Everyone in the shop including Jake had a big laugh and the incident was retold many times afterward.

My father decided to retire. The house had no mortgage, he was getting social security benefits as well as a veteran's pension and there was a small nest egg to fall back on if need be. Naturally, he conceived a plan. He always had a plan. As I have already mentioned, most of the cops in the district from the captain on down were on his payroll. Around the holidays, all the cops would be coming in for their Christmas presents. This was in addition to the regular payoffs. So what does he do? During the first week in December he's out of there. He closed the tea house and the building went up for sale. We were, by then, living in the Northeast and having no need to spend much time in South Philly he was nowhere to be found.

He accomplished what he had set out to do, i.e., save himself a couple of thousand dollars by avoiding the cops' Christmas presents. It was sort of a final victory for him, small as it was, over the police that had been a bane to his existence for a good part of his life. Eventually the magnificent property was sold for $2300.00. I mean that was the full price.

Unfortunately, the satisfaction the 'victory' brought him was short-lived, for two months later on February 9, 1955, he died. He had gotten another heart attack and was taken to the Veterans' Hospital in West Philly at his insistence. I remember they put him in a room which was then the equivalent of today's ICU. I was standing outside the door with my mother and he was waving his hand as if to say goodbye and within an hour he was dead. I know he was pleased to be in the Veterans' Hospital. He hadn't wanted to go anywhere else because it had always been a matter of pride to him that he was a war veteran.

My mother lived another 31 years and was never interested in another man. I could not figure out whether it was because all other men paled by comparison to the flamboyant Mendel or whether it was due to her old world morals or a little of both. Perhaps she thought that he was watching her from above. In any case, she led a rather quiet existence after her husband's passing. She would go on a summer vacation with her sister Lily for a week or two at the shore but did little else. And then the premature death of her son Alvin (Buddy) in 1976 really took its toll. I may be overstating it but I would guess she was in mourning until she died on June 21, 1986 at the age of 84. Her life, after Mendel's death and certainly after Buddy's passing, was devoted almost exclusively to her children and grandchildren. Her greatest fear was not of death but of becoming a burden to her children in her final years.

I can tell you that she need not have concerned herself. Rather than a bother, she was a joy to us all till the day she died. My previous comparison of her to Mother Teresa was made only partly in jest. She was adored by everyone but I must make special mention of a little episode that touched me deeply. On one of my visits to see her in the hospital I walked into the day room and found my ex-wife Rina feeding her. Rina was already remarried at that time which made the scene even more moving. I have to give praise to them both; my mother for inspiring such an act and Rina for performing it.

15

Now a bit about myself. In 1924, Little Orphan Annie first appeared in the New York Daily News, Lenin died, Coolidge was elected President and Mohandas Gandhi started his famous fast. George Gershwin debuted his Rhapsody in Blue, Metro-Goldwyn-Mayer Studios was established, Benito Mussolini came to power and restauranteur Cesar Cardini created his classic salad in Tijuana, Mexico. While the birth of a son to Mendel and Sylvia Weiss in that year may not have precipitated any world wide celebrations, I am quite prepared to testify as to the equal importance of that event.

I had a great childhood. My father was making big money and I was treated like a prince. Talk about acquiring self esteem! My grandmother, who lived with us, especially made me feel like I was royalty. Everyone called me by my Hebrew name, Eshia, or more familiarly, Eshiala. My grandmother had 16 grandchildren and most of them came, along with their parents, to our house, usually on Saturdays and holidays to visit Bubby. She would invariably prepare delicious ethnic foods such as blintzes or latkas for the grandchildren but being the apple of her eye, she would always put aside and actually hide a generous portion for her Eshiala unbeknownst to anyone else.

Those were wonderful days. When my cousins came we would have great times. I was inept at shooting marbles and I'd lose my marbles every week. But my cousin Herman (Aunt Lily's son) would come down with a new load for me every Saturday. And of course in the springtime, we'd all go out to a picnic every Sunday in Fairmount Park, right near the statue of Moses at the bottom of a place called George's Hill. My Uncles Jake, Murphy and Meyer Pete, who lived nearby, would go out early Sunday morning and reserve some benches under one of the preferred trees so that when the rest of the family arrived they would have a place to sit. The entire family (aunts,uncles, cousins and many second cousins) would spend all of Sunday there picnicking and enjoying themselves; the adults in one group, the children in theirs just like in the movies. Those were really great times. Various organizations would have picnics and they'd sell hot dogs and all kinds of sodas and ice cream. The kids would play ball and climb the trees and get dirty and it was wonderful.

A little episode in school. In second grade I had a teacher by the name of Mrs. Shusterman and she was tough. At least that's what I thought when I was seven years old. At home, my family had me convinced that I was quite a precocious kid. I always knew the answers. I read the books and I had what was close to a photographic memory. But since I was always talking in class, teacher seated me in the front row directly in front of her desk so she could keep a closer eye on me. One day she said," I am going to ask a question and those who know the answer will raise their hand."

She then asked the question and since I knew the answer, I immediately blurted it out. She approached my desk and slaped me across the face. Well! I went home and told my mother and my grandmother that Mrs. Shusterman slapped me. The next day my mother took me by the hand, went into class and slapped the aforementioned Mrs. Shusterman in the face warning her never to touch her son again. Of course, to make his royal highness feel better that night, my grandmother made a whole load of poppyseed cookies that I liked, just to ameliorate the indignity of the slap.

I had every childhood disease known to man. If today's children contracted what I had in those days, it would be on the evening news. I had diphtheria, scarlet fever, whooping cough, measles, mumps and chicken pox to say nothing of tonsilitis and infected adenoids. The summer I had the whooping cough, my father used to drive me down to Essington Avenue, near the airport where all those gasoline storage tanks are, adjacent to the Schuylkill Expressway. He would drive me through there so that I could inhale the gasoline fumes. The doctor had told him that the fumes were good for the whooping cough. So every day, when he came home from work, we'd go there and believe it or not it gave me relief.

Afterward, he would take me to what is now the Philadelphia International Airport. In those days it was known as the Philadelphia Municipal Airport. It had a wooden rail like a western ranch and we would lean on the rail and watch the planes land over us. I was mesmerized. I suppose it was then that I first became fascinated with airplanes. We used to stay there until dark. I have to guess that he secretly enjoyed it as well. Of course, this was the early 30s and almost all the planes were DC-3's. The more enchanted I became with the planes, the more my father would take me because he knew it was my big thing. Anything for Eshia. Looking at the Philadelphia International Airport today it would be difficult to imagine that it once looked like a farm. It was mostly grass, it had a small building that sufficed as a terminal and a runway and that was it.

FLASHBACK! When we still lived on Eighth Street and I was less than three years old, I underwent brain surgery. My father had removed the front passenger seat of the two-door car which folded over to allow access to the rear. The reason for this was that he could carry more cans of whiskey with the front seat removed. It was a Sunday afternoon and my father decided to take my cousins and me for a ride. So my cousins Beatrice, Gittle and Ruthie and I sat in the back seat with me on the right-hand side directly behind the empty front passenger space. It was empty but for a crank handle on the floor of the passenger footwell. In those days, one had to keep a crank handle available because of the necessity of having to crank the cars to get them started most of the time. Newfangled self starters were rather tempermental and worked only when they felt like it.

So we go for a ride laughing and singing and having a great time. Of course there were no seat belts. Suddenly my father jams on the brakes to avoid another car. I fly forward and hit my head on the crank handle. Naturally I started to bleed profusely. My father rushed me home and they called our family doctor, a Dr. Ginsberg, who decided that I must have an operation, the type of which I don't know till this day. I believe my brain was jarred from its seat. Do I have to mention that poor Mendel was in Bubby's dog house for quite some time afterwards?

Well, they get a professor (in today's terms, a specialist) to do the surgery. But my grandmother, who was living with us, refused to let the brain surgeon operate on his royal highness without Dr. Ginsberg, our family doctor, being present in the operating room. In any case, the operation seemed to have turned out OK, although there are those, I'm sure, who would question my lucidity.

I must confess that that wasn't the only time I was clobbered on the head. My Aunt Lily had married Harry Forbes who used to let me crack his knuckles everytime I saw him. The Forbes family lived in New York for a while and our family drove up to visit with them one weekend. My cousin Ruthie had a little red metal wagon and she insisted on giving me a ride in it. Under the apartment building in which they lived there was a ramp that sloped down from the sidewalk to a garage, the door to which was, of course, closed. So now Ruthie (she was 2 or 3 years younger than I) took me for a ride in the wagon and pulled me until we got to the top of the ramp. She decided to give me a real thrill, pointed the wagon down the ramp and gave me a shove. I went flying down the incline and the handle of the wagon hit the garage door, bounced back and hit me on the forehead. The metal handle was sharp and as I mentioned previously, a head wound bleeds bounteously. The blood was just pouring out, my face became covered with blood and of course, Ruthie started to scream and cry at the same time.

We tried to get into the building through a foyer that had two doors. The outer door was unlocked but the inside door was not. It had a directory on which were buttons that had to be pushed so that the occupant could buzz you in. Simple, right? Wrong! My face was covered with blood so that I couldn't see and cousin Ruthie is hysterical. When I remember this incident it always brings to mind the movie with Gene Wilder and Richard Pryor where one is blind and the other is deaf. Well, another tenant finally showed up and let us in. I honestly don't remember much more of the episode, but I evidently survived, my head bloody but unbowed.

16

It was the early 30s and we were living at Fifth and Shunk Sts. We had a dog, Fluffy, a cat and a canary all at the same time. The dog was a mongrel and he was never allowed in the house, strange as that might seem to all you dog afficionados. We had a dog house for him in the back yard and he was a great watch dog, barking whenever a stranger appeared but frightened of other dogs. Our cat was really the heroine of what could best be called a weird situation and I wouldn't blame anyone for not believing what I am about to tell you. I'm sure I wouldn't if I hadn't witnessed it myself. Whenever stray dogs would come around and seemed to threaten Fluffy, the cat would scare them away. She would arch her back and make hissing sounds and those dogs ran for cover. It was a pretty smart cat and every Easter she would give birth to kittens in our cellar by the coal heater. We would give them to neighbors and friends who wanted them.

By the way, the coal heater was used for lots of things other than heat. For example, in the winter we would wrap herrings in newspaper, put them on top of the burning coals for a little while until they were cooked. I can assure you that you haven't lived until you've eaten those herrings along with boiled potatoes and sour tomatoes from the barrel in the back yard. The juice from the barrel (russel) was also a treat. I can also guaratee that in today's world your cardiologist would have a major stroke if he knew the amount of salt you were putting in your body with these delicacies.

Lest we forget the canary, I must reveal this little episode. One of my father's pleasures was to come down stairs in the morning, open the canary's cage and let the bird fly around the house for a short time. He would then make some sort of whistling sounds and the canary would come to rest on his finger after which he would put the bird back in its cage. The canary would sing and my father left for work with a smile on his face. One fateful day, with nobody at home except Bubby and me, the bird was giving a rather noisy performance. Bubby was having her normal daylong headache with the usual wet cloth wrapped around her head to lessen the discomfort and was in no mood for a concert. She approached the cage with a rolled up newspaper and whacked it with a healthy blow while yelling in Yiddish (freely translated), "Shut up! And go to hell!"

It is probably unnecessary for me to mention that the canary expired on the spot from a terminal case of terror and that Bubby was in Mendel's dog house for an extended period of time.

I don't want to leave the cellar (notice I do not use the word 'basement') without telling a bit more about its uses. Aside from its use as a maternity ward for the cat and a galley for some delicacies, it also served as a theater and a chemistry laboratory for me. First the theater. I rigged up some bed sheets as curtains, made a theater complete with a backstage and used orange crates for seats in the audience area. I invited all the kids in from the neighborhood for two cents each and presented a play. I wrote the play and as you may have guessed, I was producer, director, and star as well. It was a murder mystery and while I had a supporting cast of one (the murder victim), I cannot remember whether or not it was my sister Shirley whom I used from time to time in my various capers. Opening night was also closing night but since I already had the night's receipts ($.12), I considered it a smash hit.

I also recall that in the summer, after it got dark, I used to tell ghost stories to some half dozen or so kids from the neighborhood as they sat attentively on the front steps. I would make up the material as I went along telling them about haunted houses and monsters and usually scaring them enough so that some of them had trouble falling asleep. I suppose I lost the knack because these days I find it difficult to scare anyone.

And of course, the chemistry lab. There was a kid in the neighborhood (Serota by name) who was known as the mad scientist, nicknamed as such after the roles that Bela Lugosi and Boris Karloff used to play in the movies. He bought a chemistry set with his own money but his parents would not let him use it in their house. I volunteered to let him use our cellar as a laboratory. After pleading with my mother for permission, she finally relented and gave me the OK. It did not take long before we caused a small explosion and a residual obnoxious odor that lingered in the house for some time. Serota was impolitely told to leave and I was appropriately punished.

There were, in our mostly Jewish neighborhood, two Catholic and one Protestant family. The name of the Protestant family was Vile and Walter Vile, Sr. was in the trash business. In those days, it was not a highly regarded occupation but as we all know, it has become a very lucrative business. The Viles had two children, Walter, Jr., who was about my age and a blond younger daughter, Eleanor, who reminded me of those Breck shampoo ads. Of course, I was not allowed to play with Walter, Jr. for a long time but was eventually permitted to do so. Once I went into his house to play and I remember feeling as though I was committing a sin against God. Back then, when most young Jews had immigrant parents who still recalled the unhappy days of the old ghettos in Europe, the atmosphere was, as we know, quite, though not entirely, different.

I could never figure out why the Viles and the Biddings moved into an all Jewish neighborhood or if they were there first, why they didn't relocate. In one of the Catholic families, the McGonagals, the mother was Jewish, had married an Irish cop and all the kids were raised as Catholics. The Viles got along better with their Jewish neighbors than with the two Catholic families, the McGonagals and the Biddings. There was very little love lost between the Viles and the Biddings.

If I remember correctly, there were five McGonagal girls. I can't recall the name of the oldest but the others, in the order of age and coincidentally, comeliness was Catherine, Margaret(Mugsy), Bertha and Dotsie, the youngest and prettiest.

The Biddings had two daughters. The oldest married and we never saw much of her. But the youngest, Margie, used to hang out with us. One day we were playing school on the front steps and Margie was the teacher. The way the steps were built, you would sit on a step and about six feet away was another step facing it. Margie was sitting opposite me, wearing only a dress and panties since it was summertime. Those of you who recall those days will know that there wasn't much elastic around the leg openings in the panties to make them secure. And after a while, from repeated washing, the material stretched and became limp. So she'd sit there with her legs apart and not having elastic around her leg, the panties would hang loose. She was a couple of years older than us so I guess she had reached puberty by that time. Even to this day, I don't know whether by design or accident, we got a 'free show'. I can also assure you that I learned quite a bit about female anatomy that day although it was not the subject Margie was teaching.

A couple of years ago, I took Joshua down to Fifth and Shunk Streets to see my old neighborhood And sure enough, in the corner store, which was by then a beauty shop, I found Catherine McGonagal. She had not changed in all those years. I don't know what happened to Mugsy, but Bertha and Dotsie both married Jewish men which is not really surprising given the surroundings in which they grew up.

17

Ah, summertime in South Philly as a kid hanging out on the 'corner'. It was an exceptional, wonderful experience that cannot fairly be described. On hot nights, pulling fully clothed neighbors as well as passers-by into the spray of open fire hydrants; chocolate snowballs(chipped ice) with soft pretzels; following the ice wagon for small chunks; yelling back at the javelle water man; buck-buck at night; sneaking into the swimmies for an extra hour in the public pool; from morning till dinnertime playing half ball, strikins out, peg ball, New York baseball, Chinese hand ball, running bases, skinners and the center of our existence, our universe, the 'corner' hangout. As the motto of the South Philly Corners Association so aptly puts it," If you were there, you will never forget it. If you were not, you will never understand."

When it was bedtime we used all sorts of little tricks to avoid it such as pretending we didn't hear our parents calling us in or pleading for another 5 minutes and stretching it to a half hour. Life was good then but like most good things, it passed too quickly. And lest we forget, our corner had its share of nicknames such as Blab, Skinny, Cockie Eddie, Moonie, Toofis, Juno, Ramble, Philco, Shnuney, Stoogie, Pony, Abzo and Shitney to mention but a few.

I had my first affair when I was around 6 years old with an aggressive, worldly woman of the same age. Our tryst consisted of accompanying her behind our back fence that formed the border of the city dump and her insisting that I watch her while she pulled down her panties, squatted and urinated. And I, being the artful lover of legend, reciprocated and allowed her the same ecstasy she had furnished me. I remember her name but I don't kiss and tell. If I ever run into her, I would certainly be curious to see if she remembers our little assignations.

I first fell in love, however, with Frieda Kleiman in the third grade. She was in my class and our families summered together at Gordetzer's hotel at Florida and Pacific Aves. in Atlantic City. My favorite pastime was patting her tush at every opportunity and show off my acrobatic skills both on and off my bicycle. By coincidence, we were both selected for an accelerated class where we skipped the 4th grade. My greatest embarrassment with the Frieda affair came in Furness Junior High when she was chosen as a hallway guard and I was not. In my mind she had acquired authority over me and it was intolerable to the point that, at least on my part, the romance started to cool. Besides, in junior high she started to blossom into a woman both physically and mentally while I only progressed physically. I ran into her at a charity affair some 40 years later and we had fun reminiscing but she told me she was very sick which naturally depressed me. That was the last and only time I saw her since junior high.

18

Now, school days. In junior high school, they published a student magazine called the Touchstone once a year. I was on the staff and I wrote a story which was published in the magazine. It was about a teenager named Jimmy Allen who was to take his first solo flight in an airplane. I had never been in the air at that time, but I described his takeoff and landing quite accurately. I suppose I had read about it somewhere and along with my Walter Mitty imagination, wrote the article which appeared in the magazine. I was always intrigued by airplanes and flying.

One of the best courses I ever took was Latin. And while its too late for my sons, I sincerely hope that my grandchildren will study it. It has been of invaluable help in the study of any of the Romance languages to say nothing of being the key to proper English grammar and vocabulary. For some reason, it has always given me a good feeling to have that Latin background. I had four years of it and in my fourth year, we were reading big time stuff like the Roman poet Ovid, since we had already learned a good deal of the grammar and vocabulary by that time. I also took a half a year of French in high school. And years later, in college, I took two years of Spanish, which was a breeze, having had Latin.

My education in high school, I can tell you now with the benefit of hindsight, has to be close to an average four-year college education today. Since it was an all boys school, there were few feminine distractions. We had biology, chemistry, physics, algebra, geometry, language, art, music appreciation, various history courses as well as English literature. We studied Shakespeare under an improbable English literature devotee named Mr. Kimmelman who looked exactly like the comedic movie actor, Fred Clark. He would have us recite with animation and then explain long passages from Macbeth, Merchant of Venice and the rest. All this in high school. It was wonderful, although I didn't fully appreciate it at the time.

An interesting episode in my senior year. One of my friends then was Lou who quit school in the eleventh grade. His father was in the installment business and Lou would go to the various customers and collect their weekly payments. I frequently rode with him and we'd talk and kibbutz and so on. One day I was in a study period in the school auditorium across the corridor from the school principal, Frank Niewig. The guys got a little unruly and were throwing papers, spit balls and having a good old time. Mr. Niewig heard the ruckus and comes into the study hall. He got up on the stage and said, "Everybody here is to report back here at three o'clock when classes are over. You people will learn to behave yourselves and act like gentlemen".

Now this turn of events conflicted with an appointment I had with Louie at three o'clock to go collecting. I reasoned, 'what the hell, (I was already in twelfth grade) and they probably wouldn't take the roll anyway, there being over a hundred guys in the study class.' So at 3 o'clock instead of reporting back to the study hall, I met Louie and we went collecting on his route. I enjoyed going, you know, because we would go to different neighborhoods, stop and see girls, kibbutz and generally have a good time.

You guessed, haven't you, that Niewig did indeed take the role at 3 o'clock and the next day Harold Weiss is called down to the principal's office. This was several weeks before the end of the term and graduation. In his office he went through the usual lecture but then scared me as he said, "You're suspended for two weeks."

I was so afraid of my parents that I didn't dare let them know what had happened. During those two weeks, I'd get up every day, leave for school and come back with all the other kids in the neighborhood. For two weeks I wandered around center city, went to matinees and tried to pass the time as best I could. I was a pretty good student but missing two weeks of class was reason enough for most of my teachers to reduce my final grades a level or two. So they gave me a B or a C, where I would have gotten A's. My English teacher, Mr.Farbish, however, flunked me. Fortunately, I was able to graduate with English 7 instead of English 8 which represented the full four years of English. I shall come back to this episode and speak of its significance further on.

I had another pal in school whose name was Arnold (Bucky) Baylinson. He was in my home room and Mrs. Avis, a real sweet, gentle woman was our home room advisor. Bucky (now a Florida resident) and I would get yardsticks and duel in the back of the room like the three Musketeers and in her quiet voice she would plead with us to please settle down. We completely ignored her as we jumped on top of the desks and did acrobatics like they did in the movies when they dueled. And again she would quietly and politely ask us to settle down. Of course, we settled down only when we became too tired to go on. She was just a sweet, sweet person and a saint to have put up with us.

19

In spite of all these shenanigans, I really learned a great deal in high school but being as poor as we were, college was out of the question. I was not terribly disappointed because I really wasn't interested in college at that time. I was far more attracted by the prospect of getting a job like the other guys in the neighborhood. One of them was a foreman in a business named the American Lending Library at 8th & Columbia Aves. in north Philly and he got me a job there at the starting salary of $15.00 per week. Their business consisted of placing a book rack in retail stores like pharmacies filled with all the current best sellers. Customers would then rent these books for prices ranging from 3 cents to a nickel a day depending on how 'hot' the book was. I realize how laughable this must sound but it was quite a profitable enterprise covering most of the towns, both large and small, in the middle Atlantic states. Most people were too poor to buy best sellers when they were published but renting the latest ones for a few pennies a day was a viable alternative.

My job description was as follows. The books came in from the publishers in wooden crates and I would unpack and process them. That is to say I put a clear plastic cover on the jacket to preserve it, stamped them with our logo to show ownership and packed them in small cartons for delivery to the stores. I swept the floors and helped load the trucks that were used by the men in the field to service the 'stops' on a weekly basis.

The Philadelphia plant had two satellite branches; one in Baltimore, the other in Scranton. I would frequently be called upon to drive a truckload of new books to the branches at 3 AM on Monday mornings so the branch drivers could get started on their routes by 9 AM. I would then drive the truckload of old books back to Philly. There were no turnpikes or I-95 then and in the winter, driving through the snow and ice covered mountains to Scranton with a heavy load of books, was something only a foolish 17 year old would do for $15.00 a week.

I graduated from high school in June of 1941. We were the last class to graduate before the war. When it began, I was still working at the American Lending Library for the $15 dollars a week out of which came car fare, lunches and a little contribution back home. I continued to work there for over a year and soon the war started to dominate every aspect of life. My cousin Herman had gotten a defense job at Baldwin Locomotive Works in Essington, Pa. at great wages until he went into the service. Word got around that defense jobs were paying 3 and 4 times the going rate for a regular job. I then gave notice to the boss of the American Lending Library (Mr. Lass) who tried to convince me to stay by telling me, "Don't quit this job. If you stay with us, your job will be guaranteed when the war is over. And we'll give you a raise. We'll give you $17.50 now and another $2.50 a week in 6 months." (The starting weekly salary at Cramp Shipyard was $62.) Can you imagine me, at 18, worrying about getting a job after the war? I quit the American Lending Library forever.

Before I could get a job at Cramp Shipyard however, I had to go Mastbaum Vocational School for two months to learn shipfitting. My old friend, Stanley Sparkler and I enrolled in this school which was in a tough Irish/Polish neighborhood in the Kensington section of Philly. One day, as we were leaving on the fire escape, about 4 or 5 goyem (gentiles) cornered us and proceeded to practice that ancient pastime of beating up Jews. We fought back and yelled and screamed but still wound up with a bloody nose for me and a cut lip for Stanley before the approach of some teachers cut short that pogrom.

We finished the course in spite of this and other minor incidents (there were no anti-discrimination laws in those days) and immediately got hired by Cramp Shipyard in September, 1942 at the princely sum of $62.00 per week. Everyone who graduated from these vocational schools, was hired by the defense industries, skill and talent being the last prerequisites they looked for. Sixty-two bucks a week! Can you imagine? My weekly salary had quadrupled. We were assigned to the swing shift (4pm to midnight) and worked on cruisers, submarines and ocean-going tug boats.

Public transportation was not very good between South Philly and Port Richmond especially at midnight so with the winter approaching, I bought an old Ford Coupe for about $25. Since permanent antifreeze was either not available or too costly, most people including myself used regular alcohol from time to time but it usually boiled out. Believe it or not, it was common practice in those days to cover the front of the hood and radiator each night with a blanket to prevent it from freezing.

And so the winter passed. There was a rather gruesome episode that happened one night at the shipyard. The winter of 1942/1943 was a rather cold one. On this particular night, a worker who was working on the rear end of the cruiser Wilkes-Barre fell into the river. It was so bitter cold that he froze to death before anyone could rescue him. When the divers finally got to him they were able to attach a cable to his body. The overhead crane, which ran the entire length of the ship's way, lifted him out of the river and hauled him back to the shipyard. I shall never forget that scene. Everyone stopped working to watch the poor man go by overhead, frozen solid in a fetal position. It was tough work but the pay was good and I learned a lot about submarines, cruisers and other naval vessels.

20

Now, of course, we come World War II or as Studs Terkel labeled it in his best seller, 'The Good War'. It was so vast and limitless that there was not a person nor country on the planet that was not affected by it one way or another. It literally transformed the world forever. It introduced the atomic age to mankind and at the same time gave us penicillin. Not only was the Normandy invasion the largest military operation in the history of the world but the naval battles in the Pacific were epic in their enormity. I must say that, personally, the war was certainly the most consequential event of my life.

The war changed everything. The furthest I had ever been from Philadelphia was Washington, D.C. on a class trip in high school. Things were so different then. If the war hadn't come, I can't imagine what would have happened to me and to many, many other millions like me. I traveled and learned so much. I once figured out that during the entire war, I traveled 50,000 miles on the railroad, being transferred from one place to another.

Without minimizing the unspeakable horrors and human suffering of the war years, an event of that magnitude had to have some lighter or at least redeeming episodes. At the height of the war there were approximately 13 million Americans in the services and with that many servicemen and women there were bound to be snafus (Situation Normal, All F…. Up). Of course, there was rough duty and good duty. It mostly came down to the luck of the draw and I must confess that I drew some pretty good cards. I traveled and experienced things that, under normal circumstances, I never would have. In all honesty, it really opened up the world for me to say nothing of a college education.

It started for me with the Selective Service Act (the draft) which required every man to register when he reached 18. At 19, he became eligible for induction, so on February 24th, a day after I reached 19, I was at the draft board office wanting to know why I didn't receive my notice. They assured me it would be forthcoming and sure enough, within a week I received my 'Greetings'(this was the way the induction notice began). So on the designated day, I, along with my buddies Lou and Stanley reported for a physical examination at the Armory at 32nd and Lancaster Aves. Stanley was classified 4F because of a scar on his lung which was a result of a case of pleurisy he had suffered a few years prior. Louie and I, on the other hand, were classified 1A and as such were given the option of which branch of the services we wanted to join. While waiting in line to make our choice, Lou whispered to me, "Lets join the Marines".

Now up to this point, Lou and I were inseparable friends but my reply was, "Are you nuts? This is an opportunity to get into the Air Corps and you know how I like airplanes."

He continued to press, "C'mon, Har, nobody else on the corner is in the Marines and we'll be the only ones."

We continued to debate the issue right up to the time we were standing in front of the sergeant's desk where, in answer to his question, I answered, "Air Corps". Lou, who was next in line, said, "Marine Corps". A few days later we reported back to the Armory and after saying our tearful goodbyes with our parents, we were shipped out. Lou was shipped to Parris Island, S.C. for 3 months of boot camp in the Marines. Whether it was because of his height (about 5'7") or pure luck, Lou spent the entire war in Hawaii as a cook and baker. I, on the other hand, was trucked to the induction facility at New Cumberland, Pa., where we were given our uniforms and other paraphernalia. Two days later we were put on a troop train and so it was that on April 5, 1943 I arrived in Miami Beach for 3 weeks of basic training in the Air Corps.

During the 21 days of basic training in Miami Beach we were given all kinds of aptitude and intelligence tests to determine who would best be suited for various air crew jobs such as gunners, radio operators and so on. Becoming a radio operator on a bomber did not appeal to me and I consequently failed all the dot and dash tests. In order to be qualified for gunnery school in Denver, on the other hand, one could not be taller than 6 feet because of the small spaces they would have to fit in on a bomber. Since a rumor was circulating at the time that the average life of a tail gunner on a B-17 bomber in combat was 90 seconds, I was not overly anxious to take gunnery training. They nailed a broom stick across a doorway at exactly 6ft and you had to walk through the doorway with your body erect of course. I know this is hard to believe, but when it was my turn to walk through the doorway, being an even 6 feet tall, I stood so erect that my body must have stretched an infinitesimal amount and I failed to go through by a hair.

What I did excel in were the IQ tests. There were 64 recruits (a squadron), all from South Philly, most of whom I knew, who had been sent to this squadron for 21 days of basic training. When the 3 weeks were over, 62 of these men were shipped out to various Air Corps trade schools such as parachute, radio, gunnery, etc. Mort Kantor (now deceased) and I were kept in Miami Beach to await assignment to a university under a program called ASTP (Army Specialized Training Program) wherein recruits who scored well in various tests would be sent to college for engineering, medicine, dentistry, etc. and other professions that the service could use during a prolonged war. This, of course, meant that I would spend the war in college.

After a couple of weeks Mort shipped out to Wake Forrest College and I was the only recruit from the original group who was still in Miami Beach. I was scheduled to go to University of North Carolina but I had to wait for a new semester to begin. So, while marking time, I was assigned as a runner for the orderly room which entailed riding up and down Collins Avenue on a bicycle with a tropical pith helmet delivering messages to the drill instructors in the field. I was also given a variety of odd jobs to keep me busy while waiting. My father kept wanting to come down to visit with me and see his old pal Davie Glass and other old cronies who had moved there but I kept putting him off because I could be shipped out on 24 hours notice. This went on for four months until the end of July, much to his disappointment.

My stay in Miami Beach turned out to be a great time for a healthy 19 year old without a care in the world. Clark Gable was going through Officers Candidate School at the time and I ran into him once in Sam's tailor shop on the corner of 23rd and Collins where the GI's had their uniforms form fitted.

My father's best friend, Davie Glass, had moved to Miami Beach in 1938 and when I could get off duty, he and his family would pick me up and take me out to dinner after riding down Collins Avenue in their convertible (a big deal for me then). They once took me to a Chinese restaurant where I ate Chinese food for the first time in my life, having grown up in a kosher household. Davie really treated me royally while I was there. He and a man named Bennie Street owned the Tahiti Bar on 23rd street as well as a night club across the street called the Riptide Club. Whenever I could get some free time, Davie would take me into the Riptide, seat me at a front table and told the waitresses to give me whatever I wanted, on the house. Word soon got around that I was a special friend of the boss and the show girls would hang out at my table. At 19, I felt like pretty hot stuff.

While I'm on the subject of Miami Beach, I would like to tell you few anecdotes that will hopefully amuse you. The only hotel that was not taken over by the Air Corps was the Versailles on Collins Avenue. We would march up and down Collins Ave. in the blistering heat while the hotel guests would be sitting on the terrace of the hotel rocking to and fro in their rocking chairs. We really weren't angry about that—just envious. Bal Harbor was a swamp. Literally! We went out on bivouac there and our firing range was on the exact spot on the ocean where the Sheraton (originally the Americana) now stands. You could say that I qualified on the M1 carbine in the lobby of the Sheraton.

There was a guy in our squadron, Hershel from 3rd and Ritner, who for some unknown reason did not like to bathe. After marching and doing close order drill all day in the scorching sun, he would put on his dress uniform without showering. His green fatigues were covered with the white streaks of dried salt from the sweat that had accumulated from marching all day in 90 and 100 degree heat. We got permission from our DI to give him what was called a GI bath. His roommates, about 6 of us, dragged him into the shower, took his clothes off with him kicking and screaming and scrubbed him with a floor brush and brown GI soap until his skin was bright pink. Back home, this brown soap was known as PG floor soap. After that he was OK and he would bathe and wash his uniform regularly.

Having flat feet all of my adult life and not knowing it, I used to get calluses on my feet from marching and I would shave them off at the end of each day with a razor blade. Herb Denenberg, a neighbor from back home and who was now my roommate wrote his mother about my calluses and she, living around the corner from us, couldn't wait to tell my mother. Do I have to tell you the subject of my next letter from home? And my next telephone call?

At one point, I was quartered at the Archway Villas (presently the Carillon Hotel) which housed a Nazi nest before the war. We used to walk guard duty on the beach with live ammunition. At that particular time, the authorities were anxious about enemy submarines landing Nazi infiltrators and saboteurs on the beach. There were jetties and pilings on the beach and when the moon was shining, they appeared to be human figures. After receiving no reply to the challenge "Halt! Who goes there?", we would empty our carbines while yelling for the sergeant of the guard. Of course, the next morning, we'd find the jetties filled with lead.

21

As it turned out, by the summer of 1943, the government knew they were going to win the war and it was only a matter of time. They discontinued the ASTP program and I was shipped out to airplane mechanic's school at Gulfport Field, Mississippi, the next town to Biloxi where Neil Simon conceived 'Biloxi Blues'. My father did come to Gulfport to visit with me and got a big kick when I was able to get him a pass to come on the base. He loved that and was quite nostalgic about the army and his service in World War I as I suppose I am now about my war. The locals of Gulfport spoke with such thick southern accents that when we ate at a restaurant in town, I would have to 'translate' for my father because he couldn't understand them.

I cannot think or speak of Gulfport without telling you about Seymour (Sy) Peltzman. While attending airplane mechanic school at Gulfport Field, I became pals with some fellows from New York City. There was Abramowitz (the only Jewish motorcyclist I had ever met); Irv Hecht who was really 17 and had lied about his age; Irv Lauria, a stereotypical Brooklynite from the Williamsburg section of Brooklyn; and then there was Sy. He was married, with a baby and came from a wealthy family in Manhattan who were furriers. But Sy's claim to fame was that he was blessed or cursed (depending on one's values) with the largest genitals I had ever seen before or since on a human being. He looked like the movie star William Bendix, husky, but a lot better looking.

As luck would have it, Sy caught a really bad cold and they put him in the base hospital so that he wouldn't infect the other men in our barracks. On Sunday, we, his pals, went to visit him in the hospital. He was wearing a regulation hospital robe and there was a rather large bulge where his genitals should be. Naturally, our first reaction was, 'What happened?'

"Don't ask", he replied. "They gave me some penicillin to which I now find I'm allergic and look what happened."

Whereupon, without further ceremony, he opened his robe. Hanging there were his genitals, which in their normal state were grand, swollen to grotesque proportions. I can only compare his testicles to medium size oranges. We all had a good laugh and as you can imagine he was the subject of ribbing for a long time. He eventually regained his normal size which as I said earlier was abnormal to begin with. By the way, I still have pictures of these fellows.

22

Having now completed Airplane Mechanics School, I was assigned to a repo- depo (replacement depot) in Fresno, California where they sent all personnel who did not belong to any particular outfits. From there, the various technicians were assigned to whatever units had requested that particular specialty.

I was given ten days to report to Fresno. This was known as a ten day 'delay enroute'. In those days, most traveling was done on the railroads and it took almost day or more to travel up from Mississippi to Philly and about 85 hours to get from Philly to California. This gave me enough time to go home then get out to California. It meant about five days at home and five days traveling. As you will subsequently see, this developed into a rather amusing situation since this <u>did not count as a furlough</u>.

It was around the end of December of '43, the dead of winter and I had been away from home just a few months short of a year. I have a stripe (Private First Class), I'm in the Air Corps and I visit with a few friends that are still around. Before I went into the service I had a girl-friend, Annette. We had been pretty close and we would exchange love letters. In the course of being with my pals, they began quoting from the letters I had written Annette to my complete and painful embarrassment. As you can imagine, it didn't take me long to put an end to that romance. I ran into her many years later and hardly recognized her.

After spending several days at home, I boarded a train for Fresno, California. It took the northern route across the United States, by way of Chicago, Ogden, Utah and then over the Rocky Mountains to California. It was the dead of winter and it had snowed heavily that year to the extent that in the Rockies the snow had accumulated to over ten feet. In order to get the train over the mountains, they had a so called 'snow train' that bored a path through the snow drifts. Then they used two engines up front and one engine in the back to push the train over the steep inclines. All you could see out of the train windows was a wall of snow. To a nineteen year old who had hardly ever been out of South Philly it was quite exciting.

I finally arrived in Fresno, California and after about a week or so I got assigned to the 1st Depot Repair Squadron in San Bernardino, California (San Berdoo for short). They had no freeways then so the route from Fresno to San Berdoo was along the coastal highway. The bus ride was just as spectacular as it still is today, only more so because it was 1944 and real estate development had not yet started. Max Baer, who was the world's heavyweight champion at the time, had a brother Buddy who owned a cocktail lounge in San Berdoo. My buddies and I would hang out there and it was there that I got my first taste of tequila which became my favorite drink for a long time afterward. From time to time, we also met some celebrities who used to drop in.

It was lovely there but we didn't stay long. After a few weeks, the entire outfit was ordered to Kelly Field, Texas (San Antonio) where we became what was known as 'permanent party'. That meant that we were to man the facilities there as opposed to transients who came to Kelly for training. It was to be my home base for nineteen months.

While I was stationed there, I became pals, I mean best buddies with a fellow named Benny from Detroit. In retrospect, I would have to guess that he was mafia. Although we were both PFCs, he kept a room on a permanent basis at the Gunter Hotel, which at that time was THE hotel in San Antonio. Right in the heart of town. By the way, the Gunter Hotel is still there and in 1998 I stopped in for a visit. While it satisfied my nostalgia, most things had changed in over 50 years. You really can't go home again.

Our barracks were off the post across the road from the gate at Kelly Field which meant that we did not need a pass to leave. So we went into town almost every night and had a place to stay. Since I was

Benny's buddy, we shared the room. We would go to the hotel coffee shop in the morning and have steak and eggs for breakfast before reporting back to Kelly. They were good times.

One night we went to a dance at the USO. We were all sitting around the table drinking beer and dancing with the hostesses who were local girls. A pretty gentile girl wanted to dance with me because I'm tall and she happened to be close to 6 feet. When the dance was over, I offered to take her home to which she agreed, much to the envy of the other guys. When we got to her 'home', which was a clumsily converted garage, she invited me to stay the night. In those days an apartment was next to impossible to get. I went to bed with her and in the middle of the night, I decided to go back to my buddies. It was OK with her because she had to go to work early the next morning. As I hurriedly left in the dark, I did not see a clothesline strung across the driveway and it caught me under the chin knocking me flat on my back. I suffered a good burn on my neck and couldn't talk for three days. Of course, when I got back to the hotel, the guys went crazy. They laughed and laughed. It was, I suppose, a sort of retribution because I was the only guy who had 'scored' that night.

23

There was a regulation (or custom) in the Air Corps then, which stated that if one were stationed stateside and exhibited good behavior, one would be entitled to a furlough every six months. By this time, I had been in the service about a year and had not had a furlough yet. You will recall that the 'delay enroute' I had had did not count as a furlough. So I went home on a two-week furlough. By this time, it was summer and I decided to go down to 'the shore'(Atlantic City) for a few days. As luck would have it, I encountered a girl by the name of Claire (nicknamed Cupcake Claire) whom I had known as a teenager before the war. Her mother owned a rooming house at Oriental and Victoria Avenue uptown across the street from Linchuck's Hotel where the family used to go in the summer. As a teenager, she would play tackle football with the guys on the hot sand near the boardwalk.

She was now 22 and I have to tell you, she was a knockout. She was not only pretty, but she had the body of a showgirl. She was about two years older than I, but that didn't matter to either of us. It was wartime and we fell in love, I, at least, for the first time in my adult life. She became my wartime sweetheart. She lived in Trenton and every time I got home, I would borrow my father's car and commute there.

When I got a furlough during the summer months, I would go down to the shore because she was there. In the evening, we would stroll down the boardwalk and people would stare at her. She knew what she had and she would wear a silk jersey dress that clung to her like a wet T-shirt. She was rather wild and would do things like send me photographs of herself in provocative poses knowing I'd become a big shot in the barracks when I'd show them to my buddies. I saved the pictures for many years but I believe my wife eventually threw them away. Enough about Claire for now. There is more to tell anon.

Back at Kelly Field, after my furlough, they started us on a practical training program. This consisted of completely rebuilding a B-17 Flying Fortress that had recently crashed and was almost totally destroyed. The theory was that if you rebuilt the plane you would really become familiar with every nut and bolt. Every man was a specialist in some field, i.e., electrical, hydraulics, radio, parachutes, etc. When the plane was finally finished, an order came through from the engineering officer that all personnel who worked on the plane will fly in it. Suddenly everyone was uncharacteristically busy checking and double checking their work.

And so I had my first ever airplane ride in nothing less than a B-17 Flying Fortress. While awaiting my turn on a hot Saturday afternoon, I drank a Coke soon after having a milkshake for lunch. I was assigned to sit in the radio room, which on a Fortress was small with almost no ventilation. And it was HOT. After being aloft for about 15 minutes and bumping around pretty good, I, of course, threw up all over the radio room. The next day, Sunday, I insisted that one of my buddies, Merkey, who was a farmboy from the mid-west and had a private pilot's license, should take me flying. I rented a tiny Piper Cub and this hillbilly buddy and I took off from a grass field and chased cows for an hour. I did this, of course, so that I would not be left with a fear of flying, given my previous day's experience. I can only imagine my mother's reaction to all this had she known about it.

The brass now decided to reactivate the 1st Depot Repair Squadron and a directive came through that every outfit like ours must have at least 2 specialists in a great new fighter plane, the P-51 Mustang. As it happened, this plane was being manufactured by North American Aviation in Inglewood, California, a suburb of Los Angeles. Based on previous tests, on which another G.I. and I had apparently done well, they assigned us to the factory on temporary duty for two months for an orientation course to familiarize ourselves with the P-51.

This was duty that a G.I. dreamt about. When we weren't in classes, we were on our own. This meant eating in the civilian cafeteria, going to the Hollywood Canteen where we would dance with and be fed by the likes of Betty Grable, Hedy Lamaar and other Hollywood notables. We were treated like royalty everywhere. We were wined and dined in Hollywood's world famous restaurants and night clubs such as the Brown Derby and Earl Carroll's on Sunset Blvd. It was two months to remember.

Shortly after I returned to Kelly, my six months were up and I got another furlough. So here I am in Philly again and of course I'm commuting to Trenton to see Claire and we had a ball. Soon after I came back from leave, another directive was published. This was around the end of 1944 and the new B-29 Super Fortress made its appearance. The directive specified that every outfit had to have two specialists on the R-3350 engine, which were the engines on the B-29. The Wright Cyclone Engine Factory that manufactured this engine was in Paterson, New Jersey. Do I have to tell you whom they assigned to an orientation course at the factory?

Some of the guys began to complain about why Weiss is always being sent to school with the desirable duty it entailed. The officers didn't want to imply that the others might not do so well in school so they answered that he's the only guy we can spare and that you men are needed to get their important work done.

So off I went to Paterson, N.J. with a buddy, Irving Luria. As I mentioned previously, Irv's home was in the Williamsburg section of Brooklyn. He took me to his home there on several occasions where I met his wife and had several home cooked meals. We would go into Manhattan several nights a week but on weekends, of course, I would go home to Philly and then Trenton to see Claire. All in all, I would say that I had a delightful two months of detached duty in Paterson.

A unique and completely unexpected as well as amusing situation arose around this time. Between the delay enroute I had gotten earlier, the Paterson assignment and the furloughs that I was entitled to every six months, I was home every couple of months at this point in time. However, to some of the neighbors it seemed liked I was coming home every week or so. They had sons in the service who rarely got home for one reason or another and they talked among themselves about how, with Mendel's connections, no son of his is going to be stationed far from home let alone be sent overseas. It was, of course, impossible to explain to these yentas that Mendel had nothing to do with the circumstances.

24

I t was now 1945. Germany had surrendered but we were still at war with Japan in the Pacific. The pattern for taking some of the enemy held islands was that the Marines landed first and neutralized them. Then the Navy CBs (construction battalions) would land, build an airstrip and put up some structures for use as barracks, airplane hangers, etc. When everything was finished, a rear echelon outfit like ours, with no combat training to speak of, would then land and man the machine shops, propeller shops and so on.

Timing, as we all know, is everything. On one occasion, according to what we were told, the brass got their dates mixed up and a depot repair squadron like ours landed on Tinian in the Mariannas a week early, prior to a landing by the Marines. Needless to say they got slaughtered. Tinian was eventually captured and was used as a B-29 base. This was the island from which the B-29 (the Enola Gay) took off to drop the atom bombs on Japan. On August 14, 1945 the Japanese surrendered and the formal articles of surrender were signed in Tokyo Bay on September 2nd aboard the battleship Missouri.

What was needed now was an Army of Occupation to man the island and relieve the men who had been there for some time. Naturally, they reached down to Kelly and picked my unit, the 1st Depot Repair Squadron. This meant that we could look forward to about two years of occupation duty overseas after the war while all our buddies from back home were becoming civilians. It would be a gross understatement to say that we were inconsolable. We shipped out to the POE (port of embarkation) in Seattle and boarded a 'Liberty' ship, the SS Sacajawea, so named for the Indian princess who guided Lewis and Clark on their expedition. As you can imagine we soon renamed this luxury liner the Sack of Sh—.

And so it was that on September 1, 1945 we sailed up Puget Sound and onto the broad Pacific for Tinian in the Marianas. This was my first time on the ocean and I was really sick. After 2 days, however, I got my 'sea legs' and even though we experienced some pretty rough weather, it never bothered me the rest of the voyage. I was able to go below and eat in the ship's galley and go about the ship actually enjoying the cruise.

There was one amusing episode worth mentioning that was not so humorous at the time. My bunk was attached to the drive shaft housing which ran from the engine room to the propellers in the stern of the ship along the keel as far down as one could get. We ran into a heavy sea one night and what would happen was that each time the ship would pitch, the bow of the ship would dip and the stern and the propellers would rise out of the sea and spin furiously, there being no resistance. Then as it pitched in the opposite direction, the propellers would slam into the sea as if it had hit a concrete highway. Since my bunk was welded to the housing, I felt the vibration and jarring worse than anyone else on the ship. It kept me up all night but since we were sailing into warmer conditions, I slept on deck for the rest of the trip. The rest of the trip being this. We were supposed to dock in Hawaii after 7 days to get more supplies, refuel and then continue on to Tinian. We would be getting a day or two off the ship in Oahu, where I was to meet Lou who was stationed in Honolulu and was going to show me the island. But as the old adage goes about the best laid plans of mice and men etc., the fickle finger of fate took a hand in our plans. On the afternoon before we were to dock in Oahu, there was an announcement on the ship's loudspeakers which blared out, "Now hear this! We have just received orders to return to Seattle and are now proceeding on our way".

The immediate reaction amongst the men was one of disbelief or that the ship's Navy personnel was having a bit of a joke with us Air Corps types. It was a cloudy day so there was no reference one could make to the sun. Everyone then rushed aft to the stern of the ship and sure enough the wake was a U. We had turned around one day out of Hawaii and were going back to Seattle. That meant that we would have been at sea for 13 days without seeing land on this unappetizing troop transport. Needless to say, everybody was ecstatic. They broke open the hold and started throwing oranges at the seagulls who were Hawaiian based birds since we were pretty close to the islands at that point. BOTTOM LINE—we were on our way back to the states !!

It is said that timing is everything and I am a believer. Now that the war was over, the boys were coming home. And what troopship do you suppose was the first to return from overseas after the war? You guessed it! That dauntless Liberty Ship, the Sacajawea! So it was on the 14th day of September, 1945 the first troop ship to return from overseas after the war tied up to the dock in Seattle. It was just 13 days since General MacArthur and the Japanese had signed the formal surrender on the Missouri and there we were—the conquering heroes—coming down the gangplank onto the pier. Can you picture the welcome we received? As far as they were concerned, the war was over and we were the first troops to return from overseas. The euphoria that resulted from the war's end was still pandemic and as you might imagine, we got a tumultuous reception. The mayor, the congressmen, half the population of Seattle, every school band, the Red Cross, the Blue Cross, the Green Cross; everybody was on that dock to greet us. There were only 900 of us and when we walked down that gangplank, Seattle was ours. We could have committed felonious crimes and would not have been arrested. What they didn't know was that we had left just two weeks earlier. Nothing was too good for us. There was all kinds of foods. The women were hugging and kissing us with all sorts of invitations to parties and whatnot. The welcome we received that day was staggering.

We were soon sent back to Kelly where our greeting was not quite the same. We had traveled 9000 miles to wind up on the north end of the field. When we left, we had been quartered on the south side. We were the only GI's (900 of us) in the entire war that could brag about a

13 day roundtrip in the Pacific. By the way, I received two weeks overseas pay while I was out of the United States as well as overseas mustering out pay when I was discharged. I was also entitled to join the VFW (Veterans of Foreign Wars) which I did for a short time to please my father, who, as you know, was also a war veteran. I think he had some political connections at the VFW post that he belonged to. By the way, I have newspaper articles that document some of these stories as well as pictures of some of the guys and the various camps I was in and so on. The newspaper articles reporting this unique event are in the WW II Archives in the Library of Congress.

25

As if this experience wasn't bizarre enough, we now come to what is probably the most extraordinary episode of my military career. We were back at Kelly Field and now that the war was over, the First Depot Repair Squadron was dismantled and they began to discharge the "citizen" soldiers using a point system. The points were calculated in the following manner. A GI rated a point for every month that he was in the service with an additional point for each month served overseas. At that moment in time, anyone with 36 points was not being shipped overseas and was kept stateside to await discharge. I only had 31. You must remember that this was late September, 1945. The war was over and the boys were being sent home.

Except for me. A few other lucky guys and I get assigned to the Pacific Army of Occupation and this time I am sent to the P.O.E. near San Francisco to await embarkation. I was quartered in a staging area adjacent to a small town called Pittsburgh outside of Frisco. It was generally known that if you were sent overseas then, it would be for a minimum of one year. You can only imagine my feelings at that moment knowing that all my pals from the 'corner' would be home and I would be on some god forsaken island in the Pacific. The Air Corps had almost 3 years to do with me what they wanted but at this time, the war was over and I wanted to go home.

Now for the good part. I called my father and explained the situation to him; the point system, my imminent departure, etc. I went on to say that the only thing that could prevent my being put on the boat two days hence was a family emergency. He wrote down the particulars concerning my outfit, phone number, etc. and told me he would get back to me.

Several hours later I was told to report to my Commanding Officer in the orderly room. "Weiss reporting as ordered, Sir" I said.

He replied, "Weiss, I'm afraid I have some disturbing news. Your father is very sick. The doctor said that your father has had a heart episode and recommended that you come home to see him. You are entitled to an emergency leave if you so desire. The C.O. continued, "You know, Weiss, it's not really necessary. As you know, your outfit is leaving tomorrow with all your buddies and I would think you'd want to be with them. Your father is not on his death bed. He just happens to be sick."

Without hesitation, I replied, "I love my father very much and I'm sure he would want to see me. Only God knows what can happen to him and I want to see him."

Now the CO is a bit upset with me. He comes back with, "Your outfit is leaving tomorrow with all you buddies. Where's your Esprit de Corps? I mean, your father is not dying. He's not critical."

I am adamant. I insist, "I don't care. I want to see him."

Seeing he wasn't going to change my mind, he told the clerk to issue emergency leave papers for me and my ship left without me. What had happened was this. One of my father's customers in the tea room was a local doctor by the name of Rubin who lived nearby. Mendel had gone to Dr. Rubin's office immediately after the conversation with me and acquainted the good doctor with the situation. My father, as I mentioned previously, had some hypertension and related ailments but he was under a doctor's care and they were under control.

Dr. Rubin said, "Mendel, get to bed right now and stay there. I'll do the rest".

And Rubin sent a telegram to my outfit which goes to the commanding officer and I get called into the orderly room. I knew this was going to happen because my father had called me and told me what was going on.

So I received the emergency furlough and now had to find transportation. As was common practice in the Air Corps in those days, I went to the airfield to try to hitch a ride on one of the planes going east and work my way back to Philly. On the first day I couldn't get a ride. On the second day, I didn't even try because as a result of a massive campaign of letter writing by GIs to their congressmen and various columnists insisting that the point requirement be lowered, miracle of miracles, they were, that very day, dropped to 32. This meant, of course, that by the new regulation I could not be sent overseas.

Although this was great news, it created a new complication for me. I still had the furlough papers and if I went back to Philly, I would then have to come all the way back to San Francisco and further delay my discharge. I did not relish that notion. So I called my father and apprised him of events. Within a few hours, I receive a telegram telling me that Mendel's condition is greatly improved. I take the telegram to the C.O. and ask that he cancel my leave as things have changed for the better. He tells me how glad he is for my good news and sends me back to the barracks to await further orders.

I'm sure the office checked my records and discovered that I could no longer be sent overseas and I have now become a burden (extra paperwork) for any outfit to whom I was attached. And sure enough, since they couldn't send me to join my outfit (it being on the high seas), they shipped me back to Kelly.

The war was over for a while now and Kelly Field didn't want me either; they've got their own problems. So they shipped me to an airfield outside Greenville, Mississippi where I was to await transfer to a Separation Center which was backed up with literally millions of GIs being processed for discharge. Greenville in 1945 was a typical little southern, redneck town. Its Main Street ended with a levee directly on the Mississippi River. On the second night I was there I met the town belle who owned a beauty shop and we became pretty good friends during my time there. I drove a tractor- trailer and did other odd jobs until I was shipped out.

By this time I had been in the service almost 3 years and never had any problems with anti-Semitism until I arrived in Greenville. Late one night, while I was half asleep, a drunken red neck GI in a rage approached me and started screaming, "You Jew bastard, I'm going to kill you."

Luckily for all, some of the other men grabbed him and quieted him down. No one was hurt and the episode was not reported but I was sure glad to get shipped out of Greenville. Finally, I was sent to the separation center at Fort George Meade, Maryland and within three days I became a civilian. As a matter of routine practice they tried to get one to reenlist by offering promotions and other enticements but I told them it wouldn't matter if they made me a General, I wanted to go home. And so, almost three years to the day after I went into the service, I was out. Say what you will about my military service but not one single enemy plane got past San Antonio.

26

Do you remember my 2 week suspension from high school? Well the war was over and I wanted to go to college under the GI Bill. I and another ex corner bum, Harry went back to Southern High to get our transcripts for college applications. Mr. Dunlap, a former history teacher of mine was handling these requests. He said, "Boys, I am sure glad to see you. You did one hell of a job over there. What service were you fellows in?"

We started to talk about the war, having a great time and I asked if he remembered me from history class. He always had a pointer that he kept under his arm which he would use occasionally to whack an unruly kid. I would slip the pointer out from under his arm as he passed by my desk, tap him on the shoulder and throw the pointer to another kid. I was a real sweetheart of a guy. But he took it in stride and we liked him and he liked us. So now he retrieves the records and said, "Let me see what we have here. Weiss, you graduated with only English 7, didn't you? You know what? You were in the Air Corps and you did a fine job. I am grateful to all you boys and to show my appreciation, I'm going to enter a B in English 8 on your transcript."

This, of course, eliminated the need for me to make up English 8 in summer school which was a prerequisite for college entrance. As it turns out, Harry had also graduated with only English 7 but for a different reason. So he asked Dunlop for the same consideration. But Dunlap replied, "Harry, I remember you and I never liked you. Here are your records."

Which meant that he would have to make up English 8 in summer school.

27

I was home now, everything is great and I go to Trenton to see my girlfriend, Claire. All through the war, as I mentioned previously, she had been my sweetheart and we were in love. I had just turned 22 and Claire was 23 or 24. In those days, a girl that age was usually a mother or at the very least, a married woman. So, she naturally brings up the subject of marriage. After my initial shock, I said, "Haven't you heard of the GI Bill? I want to go back to school. I have no trade or skills and now I have a chance to go to college. I can't marry you while I'm going to school. I don't have any way of earning a living."

What I did not say out loud was that I had broken out in a sweat at the thought of marriage at the tender age of 22.

She replied, "Wait a minute. I can't wait four more years while you go to college. My mother and my sisters are really putting the screws to me. Look, my father will take you into the business and you will eventually take it over when he retires. You know my father does very well."

That was true. He was a manufacturer of men's clothing and had large army and navy contracts. He was one of the more successful men in Trenton. But being only 22, naturally apprehensive of marriage at that age and really wanting to go to school, I was unbending. Which is how Claire ended our romance. I must say that if those days were now, we would have lived together for a while and eventually married since we were really in love. The name Claire will surface one more time later on.

28

Now I was confronted with yet another 'crisis'. I couldn't decide what course to take in college. I had my high school transcripts (due to Mr. Dunlap's beneficence) and was ready to go. After the war, an ex-GI could have gone to almost any college, but Temple seemed like the most convenient. My mother, seeing my dilemma, said to me, "Your cousin, Nate took Accounting for a year or two before the war so why don't you start with that and if you decide on something else later on, you can switch."

Which is how I became an accountant. In retrospect I should have gone to law school. I have always loved the law in addition to the fact that my father, with his contacts could have gotten me into an important firm upon passing the bar. With the people he knew, I could have entered politics which I also liked. Oh, the road not taken! But I was 22 by then and having been in limbo for three years already, the thought of spending the next 7 years in school was not very appealing. The important thing was that I was going to college.

During the first summer, having completed my freshman year, my father got me a job as a longshoreman on the piers along Delaware Avenue. A big shot in the longshoreman's union was a frequent customer in his tearoom which as I explained earlier was anything but a tearoom. The job paid very well but the work was brutal. I was given the job of 'wood butcher' which was laughingly referred to on the union records as 'Carpenter's Assistant'. What we did was shlep square telephone poles onto a freighter and fasten them to the deck in such a manner as to create a cradle for a locomotive which was then chained to the cradle.

Slow periods in that job was filled with the task of transferring 50 and 75 pound sacks of things like flour and sugar from the trailers that pulled up alongside the ship to the loading nets which would then hoist them to the holds of the ship where a different crew would unload them. On occasion, we also erected heavy, 4" thick, lumber bulkheads along the center of a hold so that when bulk grain or wheat was carried, the ship would not list too much in heavy seas and cause the load to shift to one side or the other. Although the work precluded any need for a daily workout in a gym and paid quite well, I was delighted when classes began again in the fall.

In the summer of my sophomore year I got a job as a barker for a Thrillo game (like bingo) on Million Dollar Pier in Atlantic City. I got the job through another of my father's friend, Max (Milky) Tickner who owned the game as well as the Latin Casino night club and a substantial numbers bank in Phila. He had been a milkman hence the nickname.

My hours started at 7 PM and ended when they closed at 3 AM. My crowd of guys and girls would be waiting for me when my shift ended. We would then proceed to Missouri Avenue where there were all night food stands and gorge ourselves with hoagies, hot sausage, raw clams and corn on the cob among other goodies and party till daylight. I'm sure if I did those things now I would not live to finish this story. But those were great times and my nostalgia for those days was best expressed by Poetess Elizabeth Allen when she wrote, "Backward, turn backward, O Time in your flight and make me a child again, just for tonight".

The summer after my junior year was quite different. I was back in Atlantic City but this time as a bus boy in the Ambassador Hotel (now the Tropicana Casino) and then as a checker in their dining room. The Maitre d' Mickey was a rather unlucky gambler and as a result was heavily indebted to our friend Milky of whom I spoke previously. I'm sure you get the picture. As a checker, it was my job to see that the waitresses took out from the kitchen only what was written on their checks. This, the management decided, was necessary because in an effort to earn larger tips, they would bring extra goodies out to the guests. I soon had an arrangement with a couple of the waitresses whereby I would allow them a certain freedom of action, so to speak, for which the quid pro quo was, among other delightful rewards, steaks and lobsters, etc. for my dinners. They would serve me 'special' entrees instead of the hot dogs and meat loaf that was de rigueur for the other employees.

So far so good, as they say. However, events were conspiring to cause a tempest on my sea of tranquillity. Outrageous fortune was rearing its ugly head. I had, by this time met a beauty named Rina Rosen and was dating her back in Philly but with no 'understanding' either formal or otherwise. While working at the shore that summer, I ran into a girl whose older sister I used to date before the war. Pearl had blossomed into an olive skinned brunette resembling Tondelayo, the native seductress portrayed by Hedy Lamarr in the 1942 movie 'White Cargo'. As a matter of fact, Tondelayo became her nickname.

Now the plot thickens. We began to see each other quite frequently and were enjoying the pleasures of young passion when Rina called me and informed me that her modeling job would bring her to Atlantic City for a photo shoot. I was aghast at the prospect of these two beauties meeting each other and I had to do some fancy maneuvering to keep their paths from crossing. Trust me when I tell you that it was a miracle that they did not run into each other that day.

Somehow, Tondelayo found out about Rina and a few days later confronted me with, "No more bullshit, Harold. We've known each other since we were teenagers and we've been friends and lovers and you are graduating college next June. I realize that we've made no promises to each other but this is it. It's her or me."

Talk about a dilemma! As I mentioned before, I had known Pearl for many years. I liked her and we had had some great times together but I was in love with Rina and the choice is history. So it was in December of 1949, in my senior year at Temple and with a diamond ring I could ill afford, Rina and I became engaged.

29

Christmas day, 1950 was a special day. It was my wedding day. Rina and I were married in the basement of a Rabbi's home on old York Road. Among us all, we could not afford much more. We went on a 3 day honeymoon to New York City. We stayed at the St. Moritz on Central Park South and for the entire 3 days I had the most ferocious cold that I have had in my entire life. However, the honeymoon served it's purpose. We ate in all the well known restaurants, saw a couple of shows and it was a pleasant 3 days except that I was miserable with a cold.

At first, life was not easy. I was earning about $25.00 per week and Rina was working for the government on Wyoming Avenue checking measuring devices. In any case, the marriage was going along nicely although we were struggling. We lived with my parents for a little while and then rented an apartment for a short time on a small street just off Castor Avenue in the Oxford Circle section. We then rented an apartment on Howell Court, an apartment complex, where we met people who turned out to be lifelong friends.

After a while, I was starting to do a little better financially so we decided to have a child. We eventually bought a new house on Tustin Avenue in the Rhawnhurst section. We settled into what I would call a comfortable married life. We had two children. We spent summers at the shore and when they were old enough the boys went to overnight camp. When each boy reached 13, Rina and I sent them to overnight camp in Israel as a Bar Mitzvah present which they talk about to this day. I would venture to say that Rina and I had a better than average married life for 19 years. We had a great social life with lots of friends, parties, travel, etc.

In 1967 Rina and I decided to see Europe and visit Israel which was to be the first country on the list. Because we had small children, we decided to fly in separate planes. I was to fly out of New York on El Al airlines and Rina would fly on Pan Am from Philadelphia both planes arriving within 1 hour of each other in Tel Aviv, Israel.

While waiting for my shuttle fight to JFK, Rina and I ran into an old friend Norman Millman, a/k/a Kunzig. He was waiting to board a plane to Frankfort, Germany where he had business. We discussed our various itineraries and found that we would be in Copenhagen at the same time. We made plans to meet there for dinner and since he had been there many times previously, he offered to show us Copenhagen. We said our goodbyes and off he went.

As luck would have it, however, the 67 Arab Israeli War had broken out at the very time we were supposed to leave. On the morning of the flight my bags had been checked in and while I was waiting to board I heard my name on the loudspeaker asking me to report to the El Al desk. At the desk, the clerk told me hostilities had broken out in Israel and advised me not to go there. Being the only American citizen on the plane, I asked if they could stop me. The clerk said he could not and if I insisted on going I was certainly welcome. In my mind, I figured I'd have a little excitement in my life. I went back to the waiting area and waited to board.

About ½ hour later I heard my name again on the public address system. This time a fellow from the U.S. State Department was there and told me the same story. He advised me not to go as hostilities have broken out. This turned out to be the "6 Day War". I told him that I wanted to go anyhow and could he stop me. He said he could not stop me from boarding here, but after a 12 hr flight to Tel Aviv I would be met by U.S. State Department personnel who had the power to put me on the next plane out of Israel to the United States. Faced with a 24 hour round trip from New York to Tel Aviv and back and discretion being the better part of valor, I surrendered.

Here I was then, with my unloaded luggage and no place to go. I called my wife and told her the situation and consulted with her as to what to do now. I had 3 or 4 weeks of vacation time set aside, babysitters arranged for and the business covered. I was not going to cancel this vacation. I suggested to Rina that since we had some hotel reservations subsequent to Israel in different parts of Europe why don't we change our 1st destination to Portugal and go on from there hoping the hostilities would be over soon in Israel. I had already looked up the time schedules and found that we would arrive in Lisbon within a few minutes of each other. We would meet at the airport and since we had several days to kill before our reservation in Rome we'll play it by ear from Lisbon. The next morning, as the plane made landfall, I was excited to see the red tiles on the rooftops, my first ever glimpse of Europe. And as I entered the main terminal, there, indeed, was Rina.

We stayed at the Ritz in Lisbon which at that time was a brand new hotel and I must say it was something to see. The rooms had marble bathrooms, something we had never seen before. Pure marble, ceiling to floor. We reveled in it; after all, we were really working class people to begin with and had never seen anything like it. In any case, we saw the sights in Lisbon, went to a 'fado', which is a basement nightclub with fondue and guitar players. We then decided to go to Madrid which is a short hop. We took two different planes and arrived in Madrid within 15 minutes of each other.

On my plane was a woman who had a little too much to drink and was very friendly with everyone. She finally settled in the seat next to mine. The plane was half empty and we started a conversation from which I gathered that she was from Manhattan. We landed in Madrid, disembarked and started to walk to the other plane. I spotted my wife walking toward us accompanied by a stranger. As it turned out, this fellow happened to be this woman's husband and they too were flying on separate planes. The man was a partner in an international accounting firm and came to Madrid every year for the bull fights.

At that time, there was appearing at the Plaza de Toros (the principal bullring in Madrid) a matador named El Cordobes. He was Spain's most famous bullfighter and this particular event was like the Super Bowl of bullfighting. Our new found friends were what are called 'afficionados' meaning really fervent fans. We had a drink together and he asked us if we had ever been to a bullfight. Upon hearing that we had not, he asked us to be ready the next morning as he would pick us up. He insisted that we had to see El Cordobes in action at the Plaza de Toros.

Sure enough, the next morning they picked us up at our hotel in a stretch limo and we saw El Cordobes in action. I have movies of the bull fight. It was comparable to watching Dan Marino or Joe Namath in the Super Bowl. That night they took us to the Jockey Club for dinner which, I believe, was the 'in' club of Madrid. After dinner we went to a late night grotto were we saw Elke Summer amusing herself doing the dance with castanets and clicking the heels. All in all we had lovely time.

30

The next day we were walking along a street in Madrid trying to decide where to go now since our reservation in Rome was several days hence. We had to kill some time which we had planned to spend in Israel but couldn't because of the war. We unexpectedly found ourselves in front of a TWA agency which we entered. On the wall was a huge map of Europe. With 4 or 5 days to fill we decided to fly to Marseilles, rent a car and drive through the French and Italian Rivieras down to Rome.

While in Madrid we had tried to find a Synagogue there to no avail. We were told they were prohibited at that time and there were none to be found. Most people we had asked had never even heard the word. On the way to the airport, however, we made one last attempt by asking the taxi driver. By pure luck (and the fact that he might have been Jewish) he knew where it was and took us to an apartment building with large thick oak doors with no markings on them. We asked the driver to wait while we stood there in front of the building trying to figure out what to do. A man was approaching so I asked him if there was a Synagogue nearby. To our surprise, he answered yes and would we please follow him inside.

We boarded an old creaky elevator and went up to the top floor. We get out and in front of us were again these huge, heavy oak doors. He tapped on the door and someone opened a little peep hole (like the movie speakeasies during prohibition) to see who it was. They opened the door to let us in to a hidden Synagogue. It was quite small (no more than 25 or 30 feet long) and had the usual section for the women in the rear(Orthodox) with a small lectern containing an ornate ark that held the Torah. He then led us into an adjoining room where there was a scale model of a beautiful building. He told us that the new political regime had passed a new decree which would allow the Jews to build a new Synagogue openly. They were about to break ground and we were invited to visit it when it was built. I hope to do that in the near future. Needless to say, some of my money is in the new Synagogue.

We continued on to the airport and to our surprise there were no direct flights from Madrid to Marseilles on that day so we had to fly to Palma de Majorca first where we were obliged to spend the night in a new hotel called the Phoenix. The next morning, after a leisurely breakfast and exploring some of that beautiful island, we flew to Marseilles, rented a car and were off through the French Riviera. It was a spectacular drive especially in those days. We stopped in Nice, Cannes, St. Tropez and the rest. We ate at little country inns and finally arrived in Genoa where we turned in the car and checked into a hotel for the night.

Since we were to take a morning flight to Rome, I did not want to be in Genoa and not see what it was like. I suggested that we take a walk but Rina was just too tired and decided to take a shower and go to bed. I told her I was going to look around and would be back in a little while. I walked out of the hotel and standing about 30 ft from the hotel entrance, was this hooker. She was dressed typically the way hookers are depicted in the movies, i.e., a very short, black clinging silk dress. Of course she had a cigarette dangling out of her mouth and was twirling a little bag on the end of a long chain.

As I walked past her, she stopped me and ask me in heavily accented English if I wanted to have some fun. I decided to play along for a while and asked her how much did she charge. She quoted a very reasonable price and we started to talk. She guessed that I was an American but said she liked British men better. They are not wise guys; they take care of business and they are gone. I replied that I can't help what I am and she said OK. To entice me to close the transaction she offered to supply me with a clean towel. Since the situation was now getting earnest, I told her that I could not go that night but would meet her the next night at the same time. Of course by then I would be in Rome. I went back upstairs, told my wife about my little adventure and we shared an amusing moment.

Genoa is the Pittsburgh of Italy. It is an important industrial city, at least it was at the time. We had some problems in the morning with passports and other papers but finally wound up in Rome. We stayed at the Hassler Hotel at the top of the Spanish Steps. Since this hotel had hosted guests that included the likes of Ingrid Bergman, Harry Truman, etc., I thought the Weiss' were in a proper establishment. We did this tour of Europe right. We had dinner on their rooftop restaurant where you could see all of Rome and it was just delightful. We saw all the sights in Rome and like all tourists, bought gloves at the bottom of the Spanish Steps.

While standing at the bottom of the Steps we were approached by a red headed man (I mean bright red) trying to sell us a string of travel slides of Rome. I asked him if he was a 'landsman' which is a way of finding out if he were Jewish. In English, he said yes and we started to talk. He told us he was born in Rome and since he was about to quit for the day he invited us to go with him to the Jewish section of Rome where he lived. When we arrived there, I found it to be a decent area while still showing evidence of the ghetto that had been there since the middle ages.

At the time, I was carrying Kennedy half-dollars and cigarettes which I was using for tips because Kennedy was quite popular around the entire world and these items were more desirable than currency. A group of people had gathered around us and we exchanged stories, mostly about America and how Jews were faring there. I passed out coins to the kids and we had a really nice time. They took us inside the dome on top of the Great Synagogue of Rome and told us a rather poignant story. During the German presence (occupation) in WWII Jews were forbidden to conduct any religious services. Cleverly, however, Italian neighbors would conduct Catholic services on Friday nights and Saturday mornings (the Jewish Sabbath) downstairs in the main section of the synagogue while the Jews were up in the dome conducting theirs. The resulting din of the Catholic prayers was enough to cover the noisy praying of the Jews in the dome. Quite ingenious. Needless to say, I made a donation to the Synagogue and the local Catholic Church.

From Rome we decided to go Venice. We went by rail to Florence first and I was intrigued by the way they loaded the luggage. The porters handed the bags up through the windows to our compartment instead of bringing them in through the inside of the railcar. In Florence we saw the usual sights and then went on to Venice. There we stayed at the Danieli, a primo hotel directly on the great bay. We really did this trip first class. We had a cocktail at Harry's American Bar, took a gondola ride and did the things that tourists do there.

From Venice we went to Zurich where we stayed at the Dolder Grand Hotel which is up on the side of a mountain overlooking Lake Zurich. In order to get there from town we had to take a cable car. Once there, one could hardly fail to sense the stern, severe Prussian atmosphere of generations of the old European aristocracy which I believe still exists. During World War II this hotel had to be a favorite hangout for the elite of the Nazi party and their sympathizers. Rina and I were both a bit uncomfortable walking through the lobby and being led to our room by a bellboy. It seemed as if everyone in the lobby was staring at us.

After a few moments in our room, as we started to unpack, there was a knock on the door. I opened it to see the bellboy standing there asking, "Herr Weiss ?"

A chill ran up my spine at the word 'Herr'. He then handed me a 5 lb box of matzo and said, "This package is for you."

I told him that I had not ordered it and knew nothing about it, that it must be some mistake. He read the name on the package again but I insisted again that it was not mine and he went away leaving us in a rather uneasy state. I subsequently reasoned that it had to be a practical joke played on us by our friend, the aforementioned Kunzig, since he knew our itinerary as well as the reputation and character of the Dolder Grand.

We later took a water taxi ride on Lake Zurich and explored the city where I could not shake the feeling that every other person was a former Nazi since this is the German sector of Switzerland.

From Zurich we pushed on to Gay Paree. We Saw the Follies Bergere, dined at the Tour D'Argent, had onion soup at the Piedes de Cochon in the now defunct food distribution center and after seeing most of the highlights of the Paris we left for Copenhagen, Denmark where an adventure took place courtesy of the aforementioned Norman (Kunzig) Millman. If you recall, this was where we were to rendezvous with him.

As agreed upon previously in Philadelphia, we met with Kunzig and after dinner he took us to a nightclub called the Cockatoo Lounge. There was a dance floor surrounded by tables and chairs upon which were seated some of the most pulchritudinous young women to be found anywhere. I was following Rina and Kunzig as he led us to the bar at the far side of the room and to my astonishment, these beauties were smiling and nodding at me. Now I know I resemble Clark Gable and Tyrone Power somewhat but I was nonetheless puzzled by this attention until Kunzig, after he finished laughing, explained. They were all top of the line hookers who were permitted by the management (for a fee, I'm sure) to solicit gentlemen in a rather luxurious ambiance.

As we were having our cocktails at the bar, we struck up a conversation with one of the ladies, a fellow American who must have felt a kinship with us, as she proceeded to tell us a fantastic story. She was from Los Angeles and came to Copenhagen several months every year to work as a prostitute. She made enough money during her stay to allow her to live in grand style back in California the rest of the year. Back there, she was a paragon of virtue and would call the police if anyone dared to say an off colored word in her presence. Talk about a double life!

After this extraordinary evening, we flew to London where we hired a college student with a car who was born and raised in London. She took us on a point by point tour of the city that only a native can do during which we saw everything worth seeing. All told it was an exciting and delightful trip through Europe for 3½ weeks.

31

In the following year(1968) we went to Israel, Vienna, Prague and Russia. In Israel we hired a sabra (native) tour guide with a private car. He was about my age, spoke English fluently and took us on a journey through Israel that lasted five days. One of the places we visited was a lovely town named Safed. We met an old native couple, easily in their 80's. and began chatting in Yiddish since I could not speak Hebrew and they knew no English. At first they mistook me for a sabra (native born) as I had tanned deeply and had curly overgrown hair since I hadn't had a haircut in a while. When they discovered that I wasn't, they insisted that I move there but they refused to believe that Rina was Jewish. Altogether we had a grand old time.

We drove into the newly conquered territories in the northern part of Israel and gave a lift to an Israeli soldier who was carrying his gun with him. As we came into the town of Kinetra, there were some Arabs standing on the sidewalk. When they saw the Israeli soldier in the car with his rifle, they scattered like cockroaches when you turn on a light.

When the tour was over, our guide invited us to a hotel suite where his next client had invited him and his wife. To our surprise, the client was Dushoff, the owner of the Latin Casino. We had cocktails with him and his wife and enjoyed a pleasant evening.

During our stay in Israel we were asked several times if we were going to Russia because in 1968, visiting Russia took some boldness. When we answered them affirmatively they asked us to take along a quantity of prayer books because they were impossible to get hold of in Russia. We bought a good number of books and departed Israel. We could not go directly to Russia from Israel so we were obliged to go by way of Vienna and Prague. In Vienna we had lunch at the Sachar Hotel across the Ringstrasse from the famous Vienna Opera House.

Sitting next to us on the sidewalk terrace at the hotel were two elderly women who, to me with my Nazi paranoia, looked like concentration camp guards. They had on men's fedora hats and were very stern looking. Perhaps it was my imagination but I felt that if they had the chance they would put us on the next train to Dachau.

From Vienna we stopped in Prague and then went on to Moscow. By the way, exactly two weeks later Russian tanks rolled into Prague which signaled the end of the liberal regime in Czechoslovakia.

Aboard the Russian Aeroflot plane from Prague, they served caviar and champagne. In Moscow, we stayed at the National Hotel directly across from Red Square. This was the hotel that was seen in movies like 'Foreign Correspondent'. It was all quite exciting as it was 1968 and very few Americans traveled to Russia. The hotel was dilapidated by our standards. In our room, the beds had wooden sides like the bunk beds at kids summer camps. On every floor there was a stern looking, well fed Russian woman keeping track of who went in and out of the rooms. Since that time, of course, many new hotels have risen there.

I went down to their sundry shop in the lobby to get some candies and a newspaper. Out of nowhere, it seemed, this lovely young girl approached me and started talking to me in English. She was very friendly and asked if I had reservations in a nightclub and where I was going next. I had to suspect that she was a government agent of some sort trying to find out why we were there because not many people were visiting there at that time. When I told my wife about the incident, she agreed that the pretty young woman had to be someone assigned to monitor our movements.

Unconcerned, we went out that evening to a Russian Kretchma (night club). The entertainment there was not like ours, with singers and comedians. They had acrobats and fire eaters and things that Americans usually see at the circus. We stuffed ourselves with spoonful after spoonful of caviar and drank a fair amount of vodka. We entered the Russian subway system where a man tried to hustle us to buy rubles for U.S. dollars. Fortunately I had read about the fact that trading for dollars was a serious crime there punishable by a lengthy sentence in Siberia. Needless to say my answer was 'nyet'.

We wanted to visit the Great Synagogue of Moscow to donate the books that we had brought with us from Israel but no one seemed to know where the Synagogue was. When I asked about the Synagogue they looked at me like I was talking about the moon. We finally found a cab driver who agreed to take us there and wait for us. He had probably never been to the ghetto area of Moscow before because when we got there he started acting a little nervous. We entered and met the shames (sexton) and again had to converse in Yiddish because he did not speak English and we did not speak Russian. I told him about the prayer books but he did not want to take them, nodding instead to the racks at the back of the seats where books are usually kept. He did not know if we were sent from Moscow to spy on him which accounted for his caution. Rina had the books in a large shoulder bag and while I was conversing with the shames, she emptied her bag into the racks. We flew home from Moscow after a very exciting and interesting trip.

32

Around 1959 I ran into an old friend from South Philly, Herman. He was working for the Marine Corp. as a procurement agent and indicated they were finding it difficult to find suppliers to bid on many items the Corps. needed, probably because of the paper work and other formalities involved in submitting a bid. I sensed an opportunity and since my accounting practice was not progressing at an acceptable pace, I decided to take advantage of the situation. Just about then, my life-long friend Lou had a heart attack. He was only 37 and I felt badly for him because he would find it difficult to continue his installment business which required that he go from customer to customer to collect weekly payments on merchandise they had purchased from him. I asked him to join me in this venture and that is how Lou and I became partners. We did pretty well and it was during that time that Rina and I took the trips to Europe.

Life for my family and me had by now settled into a comfortable routine. Every summer during the 60's we would rent a house at the shore (Atlantic City). When the boys were old enough we sent them to overnight camp while my wife and I went to the shore for the summer. We were part of a fun crowd socially and we partied quite a bit. Latin dancing was the rage then and we were steady patrons at the 'in' spots such as the Submarine Room at the Traymore, Around the World Room at the President and Luigi's Gondola Room. Things went nicely for us until we parted around 1970.

I mentioned earlier that you would hear more about my wartime sweetheart. It was now in the 60s, some 20 or 25 years after the war and I was on the beach in Ventnor with my family. One of my friends came over to where I was sitting and asked, "Harold, does the name Claire mean anything to you?"

Taken aback I replied, "My God, where did you hear that name?"

She said, "Well, I recently met her and became friendly with a girl whose name was Claire. We chatted for a while and she asked me if I ever heard of a man by the name of Harold Weiss. I told her that we were good friends and we go out socially. She then told me she would like to see you."

I said, "I'd love to see her as well."

She told me that Claire would be at Lou's that night. Lou's was a popular restaurant in Ventnor a sort of hangout. I walked into Lou's that night with our crowd and I saw Cupcake Claire. To tell the truth, I would have been better off had I not seen her because I could have kept a picture of her in my mind that was just glorious. Now, after 20 odd years, time had taken its toll on her as it did with us all. Perhaps I had enhanced my memory of her too much but I was somewhat disappointed upon meeting her again as she must have been with me. Suffice it to say she was not the Claire I remembered all those years. So ended the story of Cupcake Claire.

In the late 60s I had gone into a business venture with my brother Buddy and his law partner. It was named National Franchise Systems and when we decided to go public, other investors bought shares in the company. We converted Wood's Bar at 13th & Market to a doughnut shop and opened a tobacco shop on 17th Street below Chestnut. Unfortunately, after a series of mishaps and bad luck, the venture became insolvent and I became penniless.

Ricky was off to NYU and Michael had another year before he started college. I moved out of the house and took an apartment at the Philadelphian in Center City. It was a sad day. I had a Cadillac and I was literally out of money to the point that I could not afford to put gas in the car. I had rented an apartment there because my brother Buddy lived there. My apartment had a card table and chairs and a bed, period. I was really in bad financial shape and not much better off mentally.

33

A long came Max. Max was a client with whom I had become pretty close over the years. Max kept an apartment in the building for the occasions when he had to stay in town for business and/or pleasure. One day he came to my apartment on a visit and we talked about his personal problems as well as mine. There were no chairs so we relaxed on the bed. In addition to a retail auto parts store in Philadelphia, he owned a wholesale/retail outlet of auto parts in a Farmers' Market in Delaware. His son, Jerry, whom I knew since he was a child, ran that business on weekends. Max told me that he was thinking of selling the business in Delaware because he wanted to retire and Jerry, being single and in his twenties, was unhappy working every weekend. By this time, I no longer had an accounting practice worth the name so I, (grabbing at a straw as the saying goes) suggested that I might be interested. He agreed that it might be an plan for me. I asked if he was serious and not to play games with me. He assured me that he was in earnest at which point I asked how much money would I need. He thought for a while and finally told me I would need $80,000. When I questioned him about how much of that was inventory, he answered that it didn't matter as he would be selling the business "lock, stock and barrel" and would want the entire amount at settlement. I tried to reason with him about counting the inventory, but he replied that $80,000. was the number, end of discussion. In addition, there was only a month to month lease that he could assign to me.

To appreciate the situation, consider this. According to the U.S. Bureau of Labor Statistics $80,000.00 in 1970 was roughly the equivalent of $350,000.00 in 2001 dollars and I did not have bubkas. Regardless, he said he was going to New Jersey the next morning and suggested I go with him to see what was going on there, which I did.

When we arrived, Max wandered through the market while I stayed in the store trying to assess the value of the operation.

Max's son Jerry was standing at the register and he was ringing the register non-stop. The money was pouring in. It seemed to me like a money machine, a veritable gold mine. Jerry asked me what I was doing there and I replied that I might possibly take over Auto Heaven, as it was known. He became quite upset, although at the time, I could not imagine why. After giving the situation a good deal of thought I reasoned that Jerry was not telling Max the kind of money the place was making or Max would not be selling it. At the very least, he would have wanted much more money. As I looked around the place, even to my inexperienced eye, I could not help but notice that all the racks, shelves and storeroom in the rear were filled with merchandise. My father once taught me never to try to outfox anyone in their own business. So I considered that even if Max was taking advantage of me, I decided to take over the business then and there and told him so. As we were driving away, Jerry was so incensed at Max that he threw an entire ring of keys at the car.

Now came the problem of raising $80,000. Since I had no money of my own, I had to borrow all of it. First I went to my estranged wife, Rina, explained the situation to her and asked if she would sign a note so that I could borrow money on our house on Tustin Street where she was living. Understanding my situation, she consented. Next, I went to my mother. Her only assets were the duplex she lived in and a small amount of cash savings that my father had left her when he died. Not being a spendthrift, she was able to get by on her Social Security payments, veteran widow's pension and a modest rental from an upstairs tenant. After informing her of my circumstances I asked if she would lend me some money. This was probably the most difficult thing I ever had to do but I was desperate. I assured her that she would be repaid no matter what.

Between my mother and my wife, I was able to raise $45,000. by borrowing on their homes. I needed $35,000 more. Where in the world was I going to get it that kind of money? I called a friend, Sam, and asked if I could see him on a matter of some importance and without hesitation he invited me to have dinner with him and his wife at their home the following night.

A butler served a simple meal after which his wife discreetly excused herself and I familiarized Sam with the dire straits I was in and that I needed another $35,000. I asked if he could lend me any part of it. He called to his wife to bring him his checkbook and to my complete astonishment wrote a check for the entire $35,000. The man saved my life and I am indebted to him forever!

I closed the deal with Max and Auto Heaven was mine. I did not guess wrong concerning the volume this business was doing. Suffice it to say that it far exceeded my expectations. Six months later, I paid off my wife, my mother, and I invited Sam and his wife out to dinner during which I gave him a check for the entire $35,000.00. My sons worked for me during their college vacations and would stay with me at the shore for the summer. I kept the business for about 6 years until about the time the boys completed their schooling after which I sold it to another merchant in the market.

One year I rented an apartment with both boys at the Ritz Hotel on Iowa Ave. in Atlantic City. I also rented one of the rolling chairs that were lined up along the railing on the boardwalk and was great for "people watching". My mother and her sister Lily came to the shore on vacation for a couple of weeks each summer. Since I did not usually go up to the chair until around 9:00p.m. (which was Aunt Lily and my mother's bedtime) I insisted that they use the chairs until they were ready for bed. The chair was available from about 5:00 p.m. until midnight. They enjoyed sitting there and my mother laughingly would tell me how this old geezer in the next chair would try to hit on her. She was funny.

One day out of sheer mischievous motivation, I got the idea to push a rolling chair along the boardwalk with tourists who wanted a ride. I got a license from city hall and asked the chair foreman for a job. He was quite puzzled and reminded me that I had just paid a lot money to rent one of the stationary chairs along the rail. But I persisted and he finally gave me the job. I started to cruise along the boardwalk and decided to stop in front of my stationery chair where my mother and Aunt Lillie were sitting. They looked at me like I had just dropped in from Mars. I told them to get into my chair and I took them for a ride. I paid for their ride of course and they got a real kick out of it.

One night I was cruising along the boardwalk when I spotted an old friend, Sherman, who was taking a stroll on the boards. He saw me and his mouth dropped open in bewilderment as he didn't know what to think. He had always thought that I was in pretty good financial shape and here I was in the rather demeaning job of pushing a rolling chair. It was embarrassing for him to look me in the eye. He laughed nervously and suggested that I might be playing some kind of joke. I sternly admonished him by telling him that I didn't come to where he was trying to make a living and laugh at what he was doing. I did learn a bit about human behavior.

One night, I picked up an unmarried couple and was able to overhear him trying to impress her. When they get off the chair she wandered over to look in the windows of one of the shops while paid me. Out of her sight and earshot he gave me a 50 cent tip. I had a fun time with the chairs.

34

The work and hours involved in operating Auto Heaven were difficult and fatiguing but I managed to save some capital which I
decided to invest in some seashore real estate. As luck would have it, I
stayed with the boys one summer at Claire and Manny Solomon's
place, the Strand Motel which is presently the Hilton Casino. One
night I was sitting at the bar and who should walk in but my father's
old friend Willie, of whom I spoke previously. He had been one of my
father's good friends as well as a top member of the so called "Jewish
Mafia" in the Philadelphia area. My father had long since passed away
by then, but Willie (who was by this time in his 80s) and I started to
talk about the old days. Whenever my father's name got into the conversation he became maudlin and tears would come to his eyes. We
finally got to the point where we discussed local politics. This was the
summer of 1976 and I had asked him whether he thought they were
going to pass the gambling law in New Jersey. With a knowing nod he
indicated that it was in the bag—a fait accompli. The nod had spoken
volumes. Whether he really had an inside tip or if he was just guessing,
I will never know. What I did know was that people like Willie were
pals with politicians, business leaders and only god knows who else and
they certainly knew a lot more than I.

As a result of that evening's encounter, I let valor be the better part
of discretion and went on a small buying spree. I bought a property in
Northfield which is now Plaza 9. I also bought a couple of small lots in
Margate. On the advise of a friend I contacted a local realtor, Herman
Perr. He showed me several lots but none of them appealed to me until
I saw a beachfront lot that was for sale. The problem was that it was
adjacent to a house in which the owners lived and they wanted to sell

both properties as one parcel. I was not interested in the house because it was old and a bit shabby and all I wanted was the lot.

I told Perr to make them an offer for the lot only but the owners refused to separate the properties. In the back of my mind I thought that in the worse case I would buy the whole parcel then sell off the house and remain with a very desirable beachfront lot. He finally agreed to divide the property and I bought the lot. 2 weeks after settlement they passed the gambling law and the property tripled in value in one day. That was pure luck. There was a tiny bit of foresight involved but mostly it was luck.

Auto Heaven was starting to show signs of weakening and it was at that point that I decided to move down to the shore permanently. Since I now owned an exceptional lot I decided I would build a dream house on the beach and just take life easy. I started to build the house in 1976 soon after the gambling law was passed and moved down from Philly in 1977. I stayed with Auto Heaven for a short time after that and eventually sold it.

35

I hired an interior designer with whom my brother-in-law Dave did some business. I was impressed with his credentials and gave him a free hand to design the interior of the house. That was the biggest mistake I ever made in my limited building career. I let him build a fire place that took up half the downstairs area and was completely unnecessary. He created a large hole in the ceiling of the living room which accessed the master bedroom above and planted a tree that reached from the living room, through the ceiling hole into the bedroom. It had to be imported from Florida because of its size. Whatever was going on in either room could be heard in the other. It was a mess and I had allowed it because the design was so unique and he came so highly recommended. The beach house was eventually finished and I moved to the shore in 1977.

In the early 80's I hired an architect to design an office building to be built on the ground that I had bought in Northfield. At that time the local townships in the Atlantic City area still had the old building codes which were pretty liberal. They hadn't had a need to change them until gambling came along and changed everything. So we designed a 27,000 square foot office building in addition to parking that would not be possible today. Under today's building codes one would be lucky to build perhaps a third of that size. But at that time, I had gotten zoning board approval and everything was set to go except for the financing. Just then, however, interest rates rose to around 18%. At those rates the project became unfeasible. I try not to think about the fact that by more favorable timing, I would have had 27,000 feet of rentable office space. Being in the early 80's, with astronomical interest rates being the norm, I was again in the familiar position of a negative cash flow. I had these great approved plans which no one wanted to finance.

36

While sitting on the beach one day bemoaning my fate, two women came over to my chair and asked if I lived in that house, pointing to mine. When I said yes, they said that they were from Pittsburgh and were terribly embarrassed for asking but could they use my bathroom. They were strangers, but they looked clean and respectable so I led them up to the house and let them use the powder room. They came to that beach fairly often and we would chat from time to time. It soon was revealed that I had a son and she had a daughter of suitable age and maybe we can get them to meet. Sure enough, in a very subtle way, we hatched a scheme by which they would discover each other. That was the summer of 81 and miracle of miracles, in January of '82 they were married in Pittsburgh where the bride's parents hosted a magnificent banquet in celebration of the nuptials. Since Michael was employed by a local attorney they settled in Ventnor.

Around this time. I had long since forgotten about the plans for the office building because by then, the township began passing new building codes with more restrictions and building a 27,000 foot office building on my ground was out of the question. Michael had moved out, Richard was away at school and I was rattling around in this big 4 bedroom house by myself.

I had, by then, been living there for 6 years and had enjoyed the entire time what with parties, lots of company, etc. In the winter of 82-83, being by myself, I decided to sell the house. Joshua was born to Julie and Michael on the 4th of July of 83 and I made a big party at the house to celebrate my first grandchild. Then in the fall I moved to 9600 where I rented an apartment for a year before I bought one there.

Around this time the financial picture had changed and banks were knocking on my door to lend me construction money with which to develop the lot in Northfield. What a difference a year made. The building ordinances in Northfield were pretty tight by then and after consulting an architect, we decided the best way to go at that moment in time, were not offices but retail space. We created a design that received quick zoning board approval which could never happen in that space today because the codes have become even more restrictive.

A lending officer from an upstate New York bank offered to extend credit for construction money in any amount necessary. He couldn't give it to me fast enough. I hired a contractor who was recommended by the architect and we started to build Plaza 9. This was in the fall of 1984. In the middle of that winter, January to be exact, with the building less than half-way finished the contractor took off, leaving me with the project only partially complete. I didn't know which subcontractors he was using or how much he owed them. I did know that it was the middle of January, bitter cold and I was left with this partly built structure.

Since my very survival was at stake here, I started to call some contractors to find out which ones were working on Plaza 9. One led to another until I finally found out how much each contractor was owed. I was on the site every morning by 8:00am in the coldest weather that winter and little by little the building progressed. I became my own general contractor as well as my own realtor. By the time spring came, I had completely rented all the space to tenants even before the stores were ready to be occupied. Finally in the early summer of 1985, the building was completed, the tenants moved in and Plaza 9 was open for business.

37

I am a part of a unique generation. That is to say that we are the first generation born in the USA and are the link between the millions of immigrants that came over here in the 40 years from 1880 to 1920 and their descendants, the natural born Americans. It is unique in that we learned first hand the mores and customs of the old world and made the transition to modern times and the rationale and social values of our progeny.

Further, we are, as Tom Brokow called us the 'Greatest Generation'. We fought in the greatest war of all times. We secured freedom for the entire world and changed history for the next 100 years. It was a unique generation indeed.

All in all, I have had an interesting and satisfying life to this point. I have, of course, suffered a goodly portion of life's adversities but there have been some exciting if not exhilarating moments as well. I have also enjoyed the women I have known. I look forward to many more happy healthy years with enthusiasm and can only hope my progeny enjoys a life no less and hopefully much more fulfilling.

POTPOURRI

I want to write about flying, the passion of my life with which I am infatuated. In 1961 an old college buddy, Al Schultz and I bought a V-tail Beech Bonanza on which I started to take flying lessons. We sold the plane before I could get my license and as often happens, time flew by. It would be 1970 before I would begin flight training again. Still, it was one of the most meaningful and significant accomplishments of my life. Abe Stein, a WWII pilot in North Africa was my instructor. One morning, after about 15 minutes of practice flying together, we taxied up to the terminal and Abe got out of the plane and told me to go around the pattern (meaning to take off, circle the field and land). I only had about 10 or 12 hours of recent dual instruction at the time and asked him if he meant by myself. He indicated that he thought I was ready to solo. He wished me luck as he got out of the plane and I thought to myself that if it was ever going to happen, this was the time.

I taxied out to the runway, received permission from the tower and off I went. As the plane approached flying speed, I said audibly to myself, Harold, you idiot, are you nuts? But the die was cast and I lifted off, went around the pattern and landed. It was one of the most exhilarating moments of my entire life. I shut down the engine and Abe signed my log.

From that point on it was about 30 additional hours of dual instruction and solo practice until I took my test with an FAA examiner and received my final complete pilot's license, of which I am especially proud. There are very few things that I have done in my life that have been as rewarding as flying. I have owned 6 airplanes and flying has just been one of the most awesome and wonderful things in my life.

The finest plane I ever owned was a Beech Bonanza A36 which seats 6 and cruises at about 200 miles per hour. It is considered a high performance airplane and is probably the finest single engine aircraft ever built. I have flown that plane and the others with various passengers as far as Puerto Rico, Mexico and Florida many times. I have soared across the Canadian Rockies to Vancouver, island hopped in the Bahamas, flew to California twice, visited the maritime provinces of Canada, the Great Lakes, Chicago, Hot Springs and many points in between. In the Bahamas and the Caribbean, I have sunned on the pink beach at Treasure Cay, stood on the spot where Columbus first set foot in the New World on the island of San Salvador, spent time in Port-au-Prince, Haiti, stayed at the Casa de Campo in Romana, Dominican Republic, danced under the stars in Stella Maris, dined on freshly caught lobster in the Turks and Caicos Islands and flew down to Veracruz, Mexico for Carnaval to name but a few places to which I have traveled in my planes. I am wonderfully lucky inasmuch as I not only had the desire but the means and time to indulge my obsession. It was a rare combination and it opened a whole new world for me.

My love of flying has provided me with many years of excitement and gratification to say nothing of pure pleasure. It has convinced me that everyone should have an enthusiasm in life. Something that could really make them happy. Many times I take a flight for only an hour and it is like getting a 'fix'. Nothing can bother me afterwards. I find the same feeling to be true with most of the pilots that I have known over the years. Flying is a unique experience.

The first time I flew across the country, I stopped in Santa Fe and spent a couple of days with my niece Randy who lives there. My son Rick took a commercial plane from Newport Beach to Santa Fe so that he could fly back to Newport with me. It was a lovely flight and we landed Newport Beach on a beautiful afternoon. When we got out of the plane, I stood there in wonderment unable to believe that this poor delinquent from South Philly, who in his youth had gotten into all kinds of trouble, flew across the country in his own plane. It was just an incredible feeling.

◆   ◆   ◆

The World Affairs Counsel is an organization that, as their name suggests, is interested in world events and invites guest lecturers to speak, in addition to touring governmental, political and military locations. A woman I was dating was a member and asked me to join. At that particular time they were arranging VIP tours of various military installations. For me, nothing more propitious could have happened. The net result was that the ensuing couple of years made possible some really exciting and extraordinary journeys.

One of the trips took me to the Norfolk Naval Base where we explored the battleship Wisconsin. I became friendly with the captain of the ship and eventually flew back there in my plane and took him and his wife for a flight.

We had dinner in one of the homes on Admiral's Row which obviously is where the brass of the Norfolk Naval Base resides. Sitting next to me was a naval captain, the equivalent of a full colonel in the army. We were talking about flying and he told me that he was thinking about buying a small plane for himself. He was already a military pilot. I told him that I had owned several planes and I knew a bit about their values. I offered to help him find a plane, check the values and so on whenever he was ready. He thanked me with great enthusiasm and in gratitude told me he has something special for me. He told me that the next morning there was to be a lecture for our group. He continued on by telling me that he will come and signal me at the lecture because he didn't want to attract the attention of the rest of the group.

Sure enough the next day I looked up at the doorway and he was signaling me. I excused myself from the lecture and joined him. He asked me if I would like to fly an F14 Tomcat. I inquired if had taken leave of his senses. He explained that there was an F-14 simulator on the base. We drove for about 15 minutes on the base and came to this huge building. Inside there was the actual fuselage of an F14 Tomcat on a platform in this immense dark room that resembled a planetarium.

He directed me to the pilot's seat where I put on the radio head phones so that I could communicate with the controller. He closed the overhead canopy over me and disappeared. The entire room went dark as the instrument panel lights came on. The engine came to life and I was given permission to take off in this F14 Tom Cat. It costs $6,000 an hour to train a military pilot in an actual F14 while in the simulator it only costs $600.00. When the captain told me this, I commented that it is a false economy if the pilot does not experience the true feeling of being in the air with a real Tomcat. He asked me to reserve my comments until I'd flown this simulator.

I took off and here I am flying along when the controller asked me through the head phones if I would like to go after a couple of Russian MIGs? Naturally, I answered OK. I had reached an altitude of 18,000 feet when suddenly out of nowhere I spotted a target at 1:00 o'clock low (the lower right hand corner of my wind screen). He asked if I saw it and when I answered affirmatively he ordered me to take him out!

My speed was about 900 MPH and as I touched the control stick, the plane went into a diving roll. Accustomed to flying small planes I had no idea how sensitive the F14 was. Naturally the MIG got away. I was able to regain straight and level flight and presently saw another MIG at 12 o'clock at my same altitude. This time I put the target in my sights and pressed the trigger. I saw a small explosion adjacent to the MIG and had no doubt that I missed again.

I then heard the controller tell me to look down at my 11 o'clock low position to see a lake and a bridge at one end of it. He asked if I'd like to fly under that bridge. When I answered in the affirmative he told me I had to cross the lake to position myself properly to accomplish this maneuver. I dropped down to 500 feet and reducing my speed to 300 MPH I crossed the lake. As I approached the bridge, the opening under the bridge was starting to look smaller and smaller instead of getting bigger and bigger. At that instant, the feeling was so real with the roar of the engines and the bridge moving closer at breakneck speed, I barked out loud to myself, "Harold, you fool, what a fine fix you've gotten yourself into this time !"

It was so real that I broke out in a sweat and was truly panicked. But self-preservation took over, as I surged under the bridge, advanced the after-burners and shot up into the sky. When I landed I commented to the controller that I didn't hit many MIGs on that flight. He explained that the explosion I had seen was a direct hit and I had knocked a MIG out of the sky. Talk about realism! What a thrill it was! I no longer had any doubts about the quality of training the simulator provided. By the way, the Wisconsin was assigned to the Gulf war soon after I was on it.

While at the Norfolk Naval Base, we also went through the atomic submarine Hyman Rickover, named for the "father of the atomic submarine". It was a revelation to me because before the war, if you recall, I used to build submarines at a shipyard in Philly. They were powered mostly by batteries and fuel oil and were much smaller. The Rickover was roomy and bright and had an altogether different atmosphere. We also did an inspection tour of the aircraft carrier Dwight D. Eisenhower. Of course I had great conversations with many of the personnel.

The next exploit I experienced through the World Affairs Counsel was a flight to the Strategic Air Command (SAC) Headquarters at the Offutt Air Force Base in Omaha, Nebraska. We flew in a KC135 (civilian Boeing 707) which was configured as a tanker that refueled aircraft in mid-air. This eliminated the need for these planes on long range missions to make a refueling stop and waste precious time. While en route, the crew refueled a couple of planes for practice. I wandered to the rear of the plane with a movie camera and the master sergeant that operated the refueling boom asked if I wanted to take some pictures of the procedure. He was refueling a fighter plane at that moment. I positioned myself on my stomach making certain that I was properly secured so as not to fall out of the plane. As I started to roll the camera, he instructed the plane to disengage from the boom and reengage so that I could film the maneuver. It resulted in some really unique footage which I have preserved in my library.

Upon arriving at Offutt Air Force Base, we were invited to dinner by the Base Commander which he promised would be a treat for us Easterners. That night at the officers mess we were served the most delicious Omaha steaks that you could literally cut with a fork. To describe them as delectable is a gross understatement. I am told they can be purchased currently through the mail.

The next morning we were led into a huge room similar to a planetarium with countless TV monitors on the walls. This was the Strategic Air Command Center of the United States where the airborne activities in every part of the world could be monitored. SAC also maintained a 707 aircraft in the air 24 hours a day, 7 days a week, 52 weeks a year with the capability to launch an atomic missile on the President's order as a retaliatory precaution should we be an atomic target. When one plane was about to land, another would take off so that there was always a protective cover to retaliate. After exploring a huge B1 bomber we flew back to McGuire Air Force Base.

By far, the most exhilarating and thrilling trip I went on with the World Affairs Council started with a flight to the Key West Naval Air Station in Florida. We then boarded a twin engine transport plane and flew out to the aircraft carrier John F. Kennedy that was on maneuvers in the Gulf of Mexico. Since we landed on the deck of a carrier, I became an honorary tail hooker. We were on board for 24 hours going through this unbelievable warship. It is a city of over 5000 personnel. There are the sailors who actually sail the vessel, the contingent of men and women who are perform all the duties connected with air activities and of course, a detachment of Marines who are quartered separately and are the police force aboard ship. There are a number of different galleys for the different ranks and personnel, a barber shop, beauty parlor, ship's store, dental office, sick bay of course, a movie house, day rooms, exercise rooms, just name it. The ship is so huge that it is quite easy for new sailors to get lost. To say that it is an engineering marvel is not doing it justice; it simply boggles the mind.

The next day we were catapulted off the Kennedy and returned to Key West. I have to admit, after experiencing a tailhook landing and a catapult takeoff, that flight duty on a carrier is definitely a young man's job. Two weeks after we were on the Kennedy, it was ordered to the Persian Gulf. The main reason for this civilian-military program was good public relations as well as showing the public how our military dollars were being spent.

◆   ◆   ◆

Now about Nancy. I was in center city Philadelphia one day and while I was there, I thought I would stop and see Kathleen, my friend Richard's girlfriend, who was a pretty red headed colleen. She worked as a hair dresser in the beauty salon at Nan Duskins. I went into the shop and took the elevator to the second floor where the beauty salon was. I had never been there before and when I stepped off the elevator I walked straight ahead and missed the beauty salon which was directly on the left. There was a really good looking young lady walking by who seemed to be working there. I asked her where the beauty salon was and with a cute little accent directed me to it.

I met Kathleen and we were sitting around talking when I asked her who that pretty girl was. She answered that I must be talking about Nancy the French girl and offered to introduce me to her. We met and I asked her to have lunch with me. She agreed and during lunch I invited her to dinner.

We dined at an Oriental restaurant that featured belly dancers. She seemed to be ill at ease and was quiet and reserved. She had a few drinks while we watched the dancers and eventually I drove her home to the Parkway House on the Benjamin Franklin Parkway. As we drove up to her building it started to snow. I wanted to escort her into the lobby but she refused. I asked why and she answered that she was a Jehovah's Witness and did not want anyone to see that she was dating or seeing men. She did not want people to talk about her or get the wrong idea, as if seeing her to her apartment would brand her a prostitute. She tells me that she can't see me any more because she knows what dating me on a regular basis will lead to. She went on to say that she cannot give me what I am entitled to as her boyfriend or date. I then replied that if this is the way she felt, I would certainly not force her to do anything.

We then started to talk about plans for a trip that was coming up with Richard and Kathleen to fly down to Florida in my plane, spend a day or two there with his parents and then do some island hopping in the Bahamas. I said, "If you were not in the situation you are in, I would ask you to come along."

It was, by this time, snowing harder, becoming bitter cold and we were talking about island hopping in the Bahamas with the palm trees swaying in a private plane. You could have melted a rock let alone Nancy. She indicated that she would have to ask her supervisor at work if she could have the time off. When I called her the next day, she was starting to pack. Now this is a Jehovah's Witness who would not let me walk her into the lobby but she is going with me to the Bahamas.

We had a great time. Soon after we flew back she decided that she wanted to move in with me that spring which she did. We were together about a year when certain things occurred that caused us to split up.

She was a pretty good cook and first summer she lived with me Michael was also in residence as he had taken over Ricky's photo business. She soon realized that Michael liked the kind of French cooking she specialized in with lots of creams and sauces. Michael complimented her constantly and the more he praised her the more she cooked for him. I would not eat that junk, but for Michael it was great.

◆   ◆   ◆

In 1950 upon graduating from Temple University, I went to work for Jack Felzer, CPA. After working in his office for two years, I was eligible and ready to take the CPA exam. The American Institute of Certified Public Accountants had a standard CPA exam that was given in the 47 states. Pennsylvania, however, did not think that it was complex enough so it became the only state in the 48 at the time to give its own test. The CPA exam in Pennsylvania took 3½ days; 3 days covering various branches of accounting and ½ day on business law. It was given in Convention Hall in West Philadelphia. In all, 1,000 accountants took it, 700 in Philadelphia and 300 in Pittsburgh simultaneously. There were monitors in every aisle and when one had to go to the men's or ladies rooms there were monitors there as well. In the bathroom I saw one man vomiting from nervous tension I suppose and several others throwing their pencils in the air in frustration and simply walking out of the room. That year, 1952, out of the 1000 who took the exam, only 130 passed, I being one of them.

I spent about 5 years with Jack and then decided to go out on my own. Had I known then what I know now about what happened to the accounting profession, I probably would not have left accounting. Now CPA's are making important money and are being retained as consultants and business planners as well as auditors. I would have fit in very nicely. However, done is done and cannot be undone.

When I left Jack I had several clients but not enough to provide me with a decent living. My father at the time opened a variety store in a farmers' market in Yardville, NJ. When he passed away my brother, my mother and I continued to operate it. The profits were enough to put Buddy through Penn law school and helped my mother and me live a little better.

◆   ◆   ◆

THE JUVENILE DELINQUENT. As mentioned elsewhere in this story, one of my best pals as a teenager was Louie. My mother had always objected to him as a friend for me. She, in her mature and infinite wisdom, saw something in him that prompted her objections. As things turned out, she was proven to be prophetic some 30 years later.

He lived directly across the street from us and we had developed a rather close rapport. He was a year or so older than I, but when I skipped 4th grade I caught up to him in school and we were mostly in the same classes. We would create mischief together; little things like passing "dirty" notes and pictures to the girls in class. Once, after we passed a sample of our pornographic art to a couple of girls in the library, the girls turned it into the librarian who in turn called my mother. Naturally, mother blamed this outrage on Louie and forbade me to associate with him in addition to my punishment which consisted of screaming, lecturing and the embarrassment of her having seen the art work.

My father once told me that he believed everyone had a bit of larceny in them. If this is so, my pal Louie had more than his share. Here was the scion of one of the wealthier families in the neighborhood committing both petty and grand theft for some extra spending money which was invariably squandered on foolish folly. To be fair, his father Harry was, to put a generous spin on it, never free with a buck. For example, whenever Lou's father felt the need of a smoke, he would walk over to the "corner"(our universe, if you remember) and bum a cigarette from whoever was there.

ASIDE. The "corner" was such an integral and precious part of our lives that now, some 60 years later, the "South Philadelphia Corners Association" has a reunion banquet bi-annually which I have attended many times and look forward to attending again.

Not to pass over my participation in the nefarious adventures I am about to relate, I have tried, in retrospect, to figure out why I did these things. The most honest reason I could come up with, whether to my credit or shame I am not prepared to say, was that I thought it was, in today's terms, cool.

To go on. In those days of radio, almost all the houses had antennas on the roofs to get decent reception. These antennas were made of copper wire and there was a "junk yard" on 4th Street next to a synagogue where one could sell scrap by the pound like old newspapers, iron and you guessed it, copper and brass. Being creative entrepreneurs, we decided to make some extra spending money by going into the scrap copper business. Since Louie was much smaller than I and therefore more agile, he became the inside man. Understand that almost all the houses in South Philly were row houses so that to gain access to one roof was to gain access to all the roofs in the block. So one day, he climbed onto the roof of an end house and proceeded to tear out the copper antennas and toss them to me on the ground where I would compress the wires and put them into an apple basket which we had also previously commandeered. After denuding the entire row of houses, we took the booty to the junk yard, sold it and with the ill-gotten gains(2 or 3 dollars at most), went on a spending spree of movies, ice cream and such.

I suppose this would be a good a time as any to mention the fact that Louie lived in one of the victimized houses. Later, he told me that he couldn't figure out which antenna belonged to his house so he took them all. I, of course, commended him on his being able to think on his feet.

Louie was about sixteen and a half and I was fifteen and did not have my driver's license yet. On Sundays I would accompany him while he drove to West Philly and Wynnefield to collect payments for his father's installment business while I waited in the car. After a few stops, he would come back to the car with bags of lox and bagels he had stolen from a doorstep where they had been delivered by a local deli and left there for the residents.

Once, while we were walking along 7th Street, a shopping area in South Philly, which was probably the precursor of today's shopping malls, Louie steals a "schmaltz herring"(a herring packed in a thick, greasy, slimy sauce). He did this with his bare hands from a large display barrel on the sidewalk and squirrels it away inside his jacket wrapped in a newspaper he was carrying. Ugh!! He proudly tells me he was going to bring it home like any breadwinner would do. His mother, Mary, didn't quite see it the same way because when he got home, she almost crippled him with a kitchen chair.

I honestly cannot remember who came up with this next escapade, but on these Sundays, in the summertime, we would pass a section of

Fairmount Park where there were tennis courts. A short distance from the courts but out of sight, was a parking lot for the players. Most of them would remove their street clothes and leave them in the cars. We proceeded to try each car door hoping to find some unlocked. One of us was the lookout while the other took care of business. The first time we came away with over $50.00 and amounts up to a $ 100.00 on subsequent sorties. We are talking in today's values of between $1,000. and $ 2,000. Of course, we alternated Sundays so as not to establish a pattern. This went on until the weather changed and precluded further outdoor activity. We did not dare bring this plunder home as you can imagine the hazardous position it would have, especially in my case, put us in. Back at the corner, the other "Dead End Kids" wanted to know where we got the money we were so lavishly spending on them but we never told a soul and they had to satisfy themselves with being the recipients of our munificence.

And now the Pieces de Resistance. With almost all the houses in South Philly being row houses there were virtually no garages incorporated into the homes. However, there were two types available. One was known as "private garages" which were rows of individual garages with their own padlocked doors to which the renter had a key, much like today's public storage centers. The other type was known as a "public garage" which was a large one story building that would accommodate perhaps 50 cars similar to today's parking facilities but on a smaller scale. Here, a car owner would rent a space in the garage by the month and there was a watchman who would be on duty 24 hours a day. This watchman would also double as a driver who would drive the tenants home in the evening and bring the car back to the garage to park it. He would also bring the car around in the morning whereupon the tenant would drive him back to the garage and drop him off. Sort of a pickup and delivery service.

Louie's father kept his car in such a facility about four blocks from where we lived and one day he comes up with an idea to steal a car. Keep in mind that most of our "gang" were in our mid teens and did not as yet have driver's licenses but we were 'car crazy' nevertheless. So here is how it went down.

First, about three blocks from the corner, we rented a private garage across Oregon Ave. in a gentile neighborhood which was to serve as our storage facility. One night, soon after, Louie drove his father's car with Freddie (the son of a fireman) and me in it, to within view of the garage whereupon Freddie and I got out and waited until the watchman got in the car with Louie to drive him home. Freddie and I went into the garage and began a debate as to which car we should take. We quickly settled on a 1938 Oldsmobile and since all the cars had their keys in the ignitions, we simply drove the car out of the garage. We drove it to the previously rented private garage where Louie was waiting to open the doors. We shut the engine, closed and locked the garage door and walked back to the corner as if nothing had happened.

We kept the car for a week and drove it to secluded areas that we knew of so that we could take turns driving it. When we ran out of the weekly garage rent as well as gasoline money we decided to terminate the adventure. We took the car out of the garage and parked it on the street about two blocks from the corner. We started to walk to the corner and before we reached it a police tow truck was towing the Olds past us to the police station. It had probably been reported to the police and they were on the lookout for it. Luck was narrowly on our side this time.

Luck was not a lady in the next affair. About two months later as I got out of school when my classes were over and I started to walk home from South Phila. High School for boys, Louie and Massimo were waiting for me about two blocks from the school. 'Hi, fellas!' I said. 'What's happening?'

They replied, 'We filched a car this morning. You want to be in on it?'

Before I could answer, they went on to furnish me with the details. They had been walking along Snyder Ave. about a block from the school, when they saw a new maroon Packard with the keys in it, parked by the curb. They merely got in and drove it away. They had the car stored in a private garage (there is no substitute for experience) and wanted me to be a partner. Since we had gotten away with the previous caper, I suppose I felt that I had a charmed life so I became a joint venturer.

A few days later, Philadelphia was hosting one of the presidential nominating conventions at the Convention Hall in West Phila. and the newspapers needed kids to sell papers outside the hall. So we drove the Packard (taking turns at the wheel) out there and got these temporary jobs. Luck was not a lady that day, for as we got back into the car to drive home the police surrounded us. They did not take us to a police station but instead took us and the Packard back to the scene of the crime, where the owner of the car had his business, Finer Furniture Store. Mr. Finer kept us in his office under the watchful eye of his men. He rewarded the cops and told them he would file a formal complaint against us as soon as he got all the details.

After the police departed, he turned his attention on us. He was furious. He started screaming about his new Packard and raving about what he was going to do to us. He then did the most fearful thing he could possibly have done—he called my father. I would gladly have preferred that he turn me over to the gestapo for questioning. He yelled into the phone that he was going to turn the boys over to the cops if he didn't get a new car because the Packard had been dented and scratched and only God knows what else.

Luck changed her ways and did, in the end, become a lady. My father had knowledge of Mr. Finer although he had never met him. He knew that Mr. Finer, in addition to being in the furniture business, was a lavish gambler. He tells Finer to take it easy until he gets there and puts in a call to his good friend Willie, the Philadelphia boss of the Jewish mafia who tells Mendel not to worry about it. By the time Mendel got to the furniture store Mr. Finer was almost apoplectic with regret for having made such a big thing out of the situation as he only wanted to scare the kids but had no intention of having them arrested and leaving them with a police record. As to the damage to the Packard, it was only minor and since Mendel was a friend of Willie, just forget about it. As far as I was concerned, my troubles were just beginning.

Having thus settled with Finer, my father drove us home and before he got to me, he told both Lou and Massey's fathers about the events of that day. Being agile, Louie was able to dodge most of the blows aimed at him by his father and his strap. Massey was not so fortunate, as I later found out. His father almost put him in the hospital.

Believe it or not, I received the severest punishment of all and Mendel didn't lay a hand on me. GUILT! What he did was lecture me about how much embarrassment and loss of face I had now caused him in front of all his friends who would soon know about the situation. I would have much preferred that he whack me with an axe handle than see him almost reduced to tears with humiliation. The lumps would have gone away soon enough but the guilt I felt lasted a long, long time.

Whatever happened to those good old days ?

◆   ◆   ◆

During one of my visits to see my son Rick in Newport Beach, CA., we were enjoying a Sunday brunch at the Newporter Hotel. A pretty young lady, sitting with some people at the next table, sent a glass of champagne to Rick. I asked if she would join us and during the ensuing conversation she told us that she worked for Disney Studios. A brainstorm suddenly flashed through my mind.

I had always been intrigued by Alphonso Bedoya, a Mexican movie actor who played mostly bandit rolls as he did in his first American part in "The Treasure of the Sierra Madre". He was the treacherous bandit leader with the chilling smile. When surrounded by Bedoya's men who claimed to be 'Federales', a naive Bogart asks him to show his badge.

Infuriated, Bedoya yells out, "Badges? Badges? I don' ha' to show you no steekeeng badges".

At that moment he looked his most menacing and after telling the young lady all this, I offered her the following proposal. If she could get that very frame from the movie for me, I would send her and Rick to New York to see a Broadway play and pay for the round trip. She eventually did get the frame for me but could not accept the reward because of some conflict with her schedule. My friend Richard made some 8 x 11's and a poster size print which is now framed and hanging in my home as a unique part of my collection of world class art works.

0-595-23400-3